X-PLANES 1

BELL X-1

Peter E. Davies

SERIES EDITOR TONY HOLMES

OSPREY
PUBLISHING

First published in Great Britain in 2016 by Osprey Publishing,
PO Box 883, Oxford, OX1 9PL, UK
1385 Broadway, 5th Floor, New York, NY 10018, USA
E-mail: info@ospreypublishing.com

Osprey Publishing, part of Bloomsbury Publishing Plc

A CIP catalog record for this book is available from the British Library

Print ISBN: 978 1 4728 1464 7
PDF ebook ISBN: 978 1 4728 1465 4
ePub ebook ISBN: 978 1 4728 1466 1

Edited by Tony Holmes
Cover Artwork and Double Page Spread Artwork by Gareth Hector
Aircraft Profiles and Cutaways by Jim Laurier
Index by Marie-Pierre Evans
Originated by PDQ Digital Media Solutions, UK
Printed in China through World Print Ltd

16 17 18 19 20 10 9 8 7 6 5 4 3 2 1

Osprey Publishing supports the Woodland Trust, the UK's leading woodland conservation charity. Between 2014 and 2018 our donations are being spent on their Centenary Woods project in the UK.

www.ospreypublishing.com

Front Cover
Bell test pilot Chalmers "Slick" Goodlin fires up the XLR-11 rocket motor of XS-1 46-062 as it blasts away from its B-29A transporter in the spring of 1947. Goodlin made 26 flights in the aircraft, the second-highest number, completing the manufacturer's section of the trials before the program was taken over by the USAAF. Chuck Yeager then took over for the Air Force, decorating the aircraft's nose with the famous *GLAMOROUS GLENNIS* nickname in August 1947 near the beginning of his 35 flights in the XS-1 and four in the X-1A. (Cover artwork by Gareth Hector)

X PLANES

CONTENTS

CHAPTER ONE

INTRODUCTION

Capt Chuck Yeager, Lt Col Fred Ascani (deputy to Col Albert Boyd) and Maj Jack Ridley (later, chief of the Flight Test Engineering Laboratory at Edwards AFB) with an F-86 Sabre. There were persistent reports that North American Aviation test pilot George Welch had broken the sound barrier in a YF-86 weeks before Yeager's October 14, 1947 record flight, but nothing was officially recorded by Muroc's sensors until Welch was tracked at Mach 1.04 in a dive on November 13 that same year. (USAF Flight Test Center)

Capt Charles Elwood Yeager had been standing at attention for almost half an hour in front of his stern, authoritarian boss, Col Albert G. Boyd, head of the US Army Air Force's Flight Test Division at Wright Field, in Dayton, Ohio. Yeager was concerned that his recent prank, involving the insertion of small stones into the hubcaps of Boyd's brand new car to annoy the meticulous colonel, might have been detected. Instead, he was offered the possibility of a mission that Boyd described as "the most historic ride since the Wright brothers'." Boyd spoke of "incredible planes" that would travel at six times the speed of sound, atomic-powered supersonic bombers and the prospect of USAAF pilots being launched into space. The first step towards this exciting future, he said, would be the breaking of the so-called sound barrier in the Bell X-1 research aircraft. "The first pilot who goes faster than sound will be in the history books."

Even the prescient Col Boyd would have been surprised at the speed with which many of these predictions became reality. Just under 44 years after the first Wright brothers' flight, Yeager would achieve supersonic speed in October 1947, and by 1961 Capt Robert White reached Mach 6 in the North American X-15 rocket-powered research aircraft.

For Yeager, his selection for the supersonic role was the key moment in a 28-year career that eventually brought lasting international fame and promotion to Brigadier General in 1968. He completed three tours as commander of USAF squadrons with North American F-86H Sabre and F-100D Super Sabre fighters and took command of two tactical fighter wings, the 405th TFW (with whom he flew 127 combat missions, mainly in the B-57 Canberra) at Clark AFB, in the Philippines, and then the 4th TFW at Kunsan AFB, in South Korea, the latter unit being equipped with McDonnell Douglas F-4 Phantom IIs during the Vietnam War. In 1962 Yeager was appointed as the first commandant of the Aerospace Research Pilot School at Edwards AFB, California. The latter organization trained aircrew who would eventually become astronauts and space shuttle pilots.

Although Yeager regarded himself principally as a fighter pilot (during World War II he downed five Bf 109s in a single day, four Fw 190s on another occasion and an Me 262 on November 6, 1944), in his final postings he was vice commander of Strategic Air Command's 17th Air Division in West Germany at the height of the Cold War and then USAF Safety Director. However, within such a long and varied Air Force career his celebrity status derives from one flight, lasting for a few minutes over a parched Californian desert – a pyrotechnic dash in "the best damned airplane I ever flew."

The careers of Yeager and Albert Boyd spanned the years between an era of 180mph biplanes and another of double-sonic fighters and space vehicles. Boyd completed his training in 1928 and was subsequently chief engineer at Hickam Field, Hawaii, during the Pearl Harbor attacks. He then served as deputy commander of the Eighth Air Force's Service Command in Europe in 1943. As a much-lauded pilot, Boyd secured an absolute world speed record of 623.753mph in Lockheed P-80R Shooting Star 44-085200 in June 1947 while he was chief of the Flight Test Division. Known as the "father of modern test flying," Boyd was responsible for approving all new Air Force types from 1945 through to 1957.

Of all the test programs that Boyd managed, the XS-1 was probably the most memorable. This was partly because it employed the first American aircraft specifically designed and built for high-speed research, which was given an "X" designator to indicate its experimental status. Normally, manufacturers invested in the creation of new types with the ultimate aim of securing extended production as combat aircraft, based on their prototypes. Their own company test pilots conducted the bulk of the test flying, leaving the potential customers to perform their own acceptance tests.

Test pilots, both military and civil, had only been regarded as crucial participants in the evolution of new aircraft for around ten years before the XS-1 first flew. However, the enormous advances in military aviation technology made during World War II vastly increased the performance of new aircraft and, therefore, the demands on the pilots who had to prove them capable of operational use. Many of these men, like Yeager and Boyd, could draw on extensive combat experience as well as their innate piloting skills. In Yeager's case these invaluable qualities, together with long experience of practical mechanics, compensated for the lack of the college degree that was generally required for pilots tasked with performing advanced test work.

The new era of jet and rocket propulsion, swept wings and frequently broken speed and height world records during World War II and in

the 15 years afterwards caught the imagination of the public. It made new national heroes out of this generation of pilots in the USA and Europe, not least because too many perished in the relentless advances into unknown flight regimes. The complexity of the new challenges also necessitated a series of purpose-built military research aircraft extending from the early Bell rocket airplanes of the mid-1940s to the Northrop Grumman X-47B Unmanned Combat Air System of 2015. Of all these, the first and best known is still the Bell XS-1, the aircraft that first broke the "sound barrier" and opened the way to supersonic flight, with Chuck Yeager at the helm.

Col Albert G. Boyd poses in front of the P-80R that he flew on June 19, 1947 from Muroc Army Air Field to set a new world airspeed record of 623.753mph, returning the record to the United States after nearly 24 years. Col Boyd's firm, wise guidance was a vital factor in the success of the X-1 project. He joined the USAAC in 1927 and retired from the USAF in 1976, having flown 723 aircraft types for a total of 23,000 flying hours. (USAF)

CHAPTER TWO

ORIGINS

The Heinkel He 178 was the world's first turbojet technology demonstrator, having made its maiden flight just one week before the beginning of World War II. Powered by a single 992lb-thrust gas turbine designed by Dr Hans Ohain, the 400mph-plus airplane provoked little interest from within the German Air Ministry. (Osprey)

By 1942 it was clear that the propeller-driven fighter had almost reached its maximum potential speed, limited mainly by the drag caused by the propeller itself. In a test dive a Lockheed P-38E Lightning broke up on November 5, 1941 and crashed into a house near Glendale, California, killing Lockheed test pilot Ralph Virden. Wind tunnel tests by the National Advisory Committee for Aeronautics (NACA) showed that a series of shockwaves known as compressibility, caused by a pile-up of air ahead of the aircraft, had prevented the P-38E from recovering from a steep dive and torn off its entire tail assembly.

In England the Royal Aircraft Establishment's (RAE) High Speed Unit tests with a Spitfire V in 1941 had shown that it could dive to Mach 0.78, encountering greatly increased drag as it approached Mach 0.80. The highest recorded speed by a piston-engined fighter was achieved by Sqn Ldr J. R. Tobin of the RAE when he reached Mach 0.9 (615mph) in a Spitfire PR XI in 1943 while diving from 40,000ft. Sqn Ldr A. F. Martindale dived a Spitfire to Mach 0.89 (606mph) on April 27, 1944, faster than contemporary Meteor and Vampire jets, but the propeller and reduction gear broke away, coating his windshield in oil while he exerted a 100lb force on the control column to pull out. Sadly, four of the six High Speed Unit pilots who volunteered for these near-sonic flights were killed during their terminal-velocity dives.

In the USA, Republic P-47J 43-46952 achieved an unofficial speed record in level flight when it reached Mach 0.75 (504mph) on August 4, 1944. However, as with the RAE's High Speed Unit, diving tests conducted by the USAAF with the P-47, Bell P-39 Airacobra and other piston-engined types caused an alarming rate of tail failures and disintegration. Among the pilots who made high subsonic test dives in P-47s was Bob Hoover, who later became back-up XS-1 pilot to Chuck Yeager.

Pilots of the fastest propeller-driven types had often returned from combat having experienced partial loss of control in high-speed dives. Their normally docile aircraft encountered severe buffeting, vibration that made it impossible to read instruments and a powerful nose-down trim change that could lead to an unrecoverable dive or spin. Maj Pete Barsodi made power dives in his P-51 to try to identify the compressibility problem, and he actually photographed shockwaves over his aircraft's wing during one headlong plunge. The P-51 became NACA's first "flying laboratory," instrumented to obtain data that could not easily be derived from wind tunnel tests.

Dr Theodore von Kármán from the California Institute of Technology was an early advocate for a multi-slot, transonic wind tunnel in the USA. Co-founder of the Jet Propulsion Laboratory, his pioneering work on high-speed aerodynamics and aeronautical engineering greatly influenced Bell in its development of the XS-1. (USAF)

Like the RAE, NACA's Compressibility Research Division lacked wind tunnels that could simulate the effects of transonic and supersonic flight to explore these phenomena, requiring real aircraft and pilots to explore the boundaries. NACA's existing "closed throat" tunnels choked with airflow shockwaves, which bounced off the tunnel walls and back onto models at Mach 0.75 to Mach 1.3, making it impossible to simulate real high-speed flight. A more effective multi-slot, transonic tunnel (devised by NACA's Ray Wright and compressibility expert John Stack after a NACA review of wind tunnels in Europe) was not operational until 1951.

The need for such a tunnel had been advocated by Dr Theodore von Kármán from the California Institute of Technology after he attended the 1935 Volta Conference on High Speeds in Aviation. Opened by *Il Duce* Benito Mussolini, this crucial assembly in Rome of the world's foremost aeronautical designers and theoreticians had convinced many of those present that supersonic flight was a possibility, but appropriate research facilities including high-speed wind tunnels were a prerequisite.

In the same year British scientist W. F. Hilton, working at the National Physical Laboratory's wind tunnel, was interviewed about his aerofoil drag research. He remarked how the resistance of a wing increased "like a barrier" as the airflow approached supersonic levels. From this, the Press deduced the term "sound barrier," which was popularly but inaccurately attached to most subsequent discussion of the topic. It also led to a burgeoning popular Press mythology which included theories that, beyond the "sound barrier" (or "infinite drag"), pilots would experience a time reversal and return as much younger versions of themselves, lose their voices or simply dematerialize!

The development of new forms of high-speed propulsion was already progressing by the end of World War II. On May 15, 1941 the first British jet aircraft, the Gloster E.28/39, made its maiden flight using a Power Jets W.1 engine patented by Frank Whittle in 1930. It included provision for four machine guns but its speed was limited to 466mph.

1941 was also the year in which Allied intelligence was made aware of the spectacular advances in aircraft development, using jet and rocket propulsion, that were taking place in Nazi Germany. Heinkel's He 178, the world's first turbojet technology demonstrator, had flown one week before the beginning of World War II with a single 992lb-thrust gas turbine designed by Dr Hans Ohain. Although it could have exceeded 400mph, the airplane provoked little interest from within the German Air Ministry, which was focussed on building conventional aircraft for imminent war. Also, in September 1939, Messerschmitt's Dr Waldemar Voigt had begun work on the twin-jet Me 262, the first operational jet fighter. Engine development delays (like Whittle, BMW had difficulty in finding sufficiently heat-resistant metals) and Adolf Hitler's insistence on using it as a "revenge bomber" limited the airplane's considerable potential as a devastator of Allied bomber forces.

German advances in rocket propulsion would also influence American initiatives in building a supersonic research vehicle. In 1939 the Heinkel He 176 V1 was the first liquid-fuel rocket aircraft. It had a very thin, straight wing, conventional tail unit and a large faired-in canopy over the ejectable nose and cockpit section of its tiny 17ft wooden fuselage – the entire aircraft was small enough to be wind tunnel tested. Although its 1,323lb-thrust Walter HWK R1-203 hydrogen peroxide engine ran for only about a minute, it accelerated the He 176 to 500mph. Fortunately, the *Führer* decided that a developed, fighter version was unnecessary as the war would be won before it could be deployed. Another Heinkel initiative, involving pioneering rocket scientist Werner von Braun, used the fuselage of a piston-engined Heinkel He 112 fighter to ground-test a rocket motor with alcohol/liquid oxygen (lox) propellants that were pressure-fed, rather than pumped, to the combustion chambers by gas from the evaporating lox. When Bell used a similar system several years later it required a separate nitrogen pressure source.

The idea of building a transonic research craft had been suggested by John Stack as early as 1928. Ten years on, Ezra Kotcher, later head of aeronautical research at the USAAC's Wright Field Engineering

The Heinkel He 176 V1 was the first liquid-fuel rocket aircraft. Boasting a very thin, straight wing, conventional tail unit and a large faired-in canopy over the ejectable nose and cockpit section of its tiny 17ft wooden fuselage, the entire aircraft was small enough to be wind tunnel tested. Its 1,323lb thrust Walter HWK R1-203 hydrogen peroxide engine ran for only about a minute, during which time it would have accelerated the He 176 to 500mph. (EN-Archive)

School, prepared a paper advocating a transonic research program using a rocket-propelled aircraft to generate flight data that could be compared with wind tunnel findings and observations of free-fall or rocket-powered models to test aerofoil shapes. It was eventually seen by USAAF chief of staff, Maj Gen "Hap" Arnold, and subsequently triggered a 1943 request for Theodore von Kármán to investigate the possibility of an aircraft capable of Mach 1.5. Arnold had begun to realize the possibilities of advancement for military aviation, and he established the Scientific Advisory Board headed by von Kármán that drew in many acclaimed scientists. Von Kármán responded positively to Arnold's ambitious request, while John Stack at NACA's Langley, Virginia, site promoted a small Mach 1 aircraft using a license-built Whittle W.1 engine – the only practical option at the time.

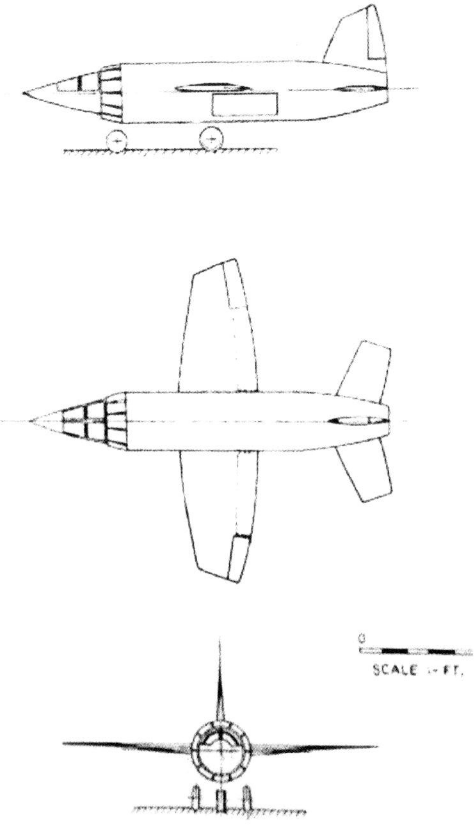

MILES M52 E 24/43

An early sketch of the Miles M.52, with its thin, straight wing, bullet-shaped fuselage and all-moving horizontal tail. Unlike the XS-1, it had an afterburning turbojet engine (with a highly innovative, airflow-slowing shock cone in the intake that also contained the cockpit) and it took off from the ground. The cancellation decision originated with Sir Ben Lockspeiser, Director-General of Scientific Air Research for the Ministry of Supply, who was convinced that the swept wing was the only solution for supersonic flight. He also believed that he could not risk the lives of test pilots in such a dangerous venture when radio-controlled models could be used instead. (Miles Aircraft)

THE BRITISH INITIATIVE

Britain's lead in jet-powered aviation in the early 1940s and captured intelligence on German aircraft projects caused the Ministry of Aircraft Production (MAP) to establish a Supersonic Committee in May 1943 under Ben Lockspeiser. It considered reports of a 1,000mph German aircraft – probably the Messerschmitt Me 163 rocket-propelled interceptor, first flown in 1941. It also debated the construction of a piloted supersonic aircraft, later outlined in MAP specification E.24/43. With a background in small piston-engined training aircraft (and a single, 12-gun fighter prototype derived from them), the Miles Aircraft Company responded to this with the M.52, the world's first supersonic research aircraft proposal and an astonishingly innovative design. Like Bell Aircraft in the USA, Miles was not over-burdened with production of wartime aircraft, freeing it for experimental projects. It was also located close to the RAE at Farnborough.

The objectives described in E.24/43 of October 1943 were speed of 1,000mph, a climb to 40,000ft and 30 minutes at this altitude at 700mph, an all-moving tailplane with no elevator and maximum weight of 6,000lb. Power was to be provided by a Whittle W.2/700 with "bypass heating," and this remarkable aircraft was to fly within nine months of initiation. Lacking sufficient data on delta or swept wings, the designers, led by chief aerodynamicist Dennis Bancroft, used a straight bi-convex (formed from opposing symmetrical arcs) wing – a type that had been tested to Mach 2.13 by Antonio Ferri in the Guidonia wind tunnel in Italy. This was the world's first supersonic wind tunnel, capable of simulating Mach 2.7 conditions. Dr Adolf Busemann, speaking at the 1935 Volta Conference, had suggested swept, or "arrow" wings to defeat the transonic shockwave and drag problem common to straight wings. He even proposed a supersonic biplane configuration to make the shockwaves cancel each other out. No detailed information on sweepback was available to the M.52 team.

The M.52's flying surfaces had razor-sharp leading edges (like the Lockheed F-104 Starfighter of 1952) and the wing, spanning 26.87ft, had a 7.5 percent thickness/chord ratio – thinner than the straight wing chosen for the Bell X-1. The semi-reclining pilot was encased in a 5ft-diameter capsule that formed a nose cone within the circular jet intake. The design's No. 4 Augmentor (reheat) unit promised at least 5,000lb of thrust. Plans included the use of turbofans in the engine, a variable-area jet nozzle and bypass ducting for ramjet effect among other features used in later designs. In an emergency the cone would be ejected by explosive bolts and slowed by a drogue parachute to enable the pilot to make a conventional bail-out. A similar system was later used in the Bell X-2, as were the bi-convex wing and all-moving, swept-back bi-convex horizontal stabilizer.

The shape of the M.52's 35ft 7in long fuselage was influenced by the considerable available data on projectiles provided by the UK's Armament Research Department and mid-1930s research by Lt Col H. Zornig in the USA. A bullet-shaped object created the least supersonic drag and gave more accuracy than other shapes – a point that was well understood by Werner von Braun. His V2 ballistic missile of 1942 was the first aerial vehicle to exceed the speed of sound, and it did so just 30 seconds after launch. Later tests in the USA showed that the missile, shaped like a giant .50-caliber bullet and evolved in German wartime supersonic wind tunnels, could reach Mach 4 – a regular occurrence for the 3,160 examples that were launched.

A small frontal area and a thin wing were about all the RAE, lacking a supersonic wind tunnel, could offer Miles as guidance for supersonic performance, together with some rather pessimistic forecasts about the difficulty of breaking the "sound barrier." However, the Aeronautical Department of the National Physical Laboratory at Teddington, with three small supersonic tunnels for ballistic tests on bullets, gave the project more positive encouragement. Bullets with an ogival (arched with a pointed tip) nose profile were able to travel at speeds in excess of 2,300mph with great stability and more accuracy than other shapes. However, none of the published data or wind tunnel capability was helpful concerning drag and compressibility in the transonic region between Mach 0.85 and 1.25.

Of all the M.52's intended innovations, the all-moving tailplane had the most far-reaching benefits, particularly for the Bell X-planes. It allowed the pilot to maintain control in the transonic regime where conventional elevators became ineffective due to disturbed airflow over the tailplane. It was certainly noted by the American team that MAP invited to Miles Aircraft in the fall of 1944. Representatives of the USAAF, NACA and Bell Aircraft were included, and MAP instructed Miles to give them full details and drawings of the M.52 project, with the idea that a reciprocal visit would occur a few weeks later to share American supersonic research data. When the return visit was cancelled by the Pentagon a week later for security reasons, many at Miles felt that the American delegation had come off rather well. It was also suggested that the Americans might not have had much to offer in exchange compared with the spectacular progress made in England.

The M.52 team pushed ahead and the first aircraft was well advanced when, on January 15, 1945, Prime Minister Winston Churchill issued a directive stating that any research and development projects that "are not likely to be used in operations on a considerable scale in the second half of 1946 should be slowed down or temporarily abandoned" to allow re-focus on post-war civilian production. This directive, combined with opposition to the project from some members of the Supersonic Committee and Whittle's resignation from his Power Jets company in January 1946 contributed to the final cancellation of the M.52 in February 1946, with the first prototype only three weeks from completion. Recent analyses of the M.52 design by Rolls-Royce have indicated that it could well have achieved at least Mach 1 in level flight. Indeed, a reduced-scale radio-controlled model attained Mach 1.38 in October 1948. Many in the UK and USA believed that its cancellation handed Britain's lead in supersonic flight research to the USA.

Geoffrey de Havilland climbs out of the cockpit of the DH 108 Swallow following a test flight during the late summer of 1946. (*Flight*)

Lacking government support, some British manufacturers actually followed a rather different route that was rather more reminiscent of their efforts towards the World Speed Record flights in the Schneider Trophy races between 1913 and 1931. Although in 1946 the Ministry of Supply announced that all future supersonic testing would be done with air-dropped models (leading to some collaborative tests with Wright Field), Geoffrey de Havilland had almost completed his DH 108 Swallow, and it was permitted to continue.

Swept-winged and tailless, the graceful Swallow was designed to explore swept-wing control issues at high speeds for the company's forthcoming Comet jet airliner. Although it would hopefully achieve a new speed record, it was not envisaged as a contender for supersonic honors. In the hands of John Derry, the third prototype did exceed Mach 1 in a dive on September 6, 1948, thus becoming the first British aircraft to do so. Geoffrey de Havilland Jr flew several practice runs below 1,100ft for the speed record attempt, but on the final run on September 27, 1946 the DH 108 entered a series of uncontrollable high-speed oscillations under compressibility at around Mach 0.88. The main spar failed, the wings broke away and the aircraft disintegrated, killing de Havilland.

This tragedy exacerbated the myth of an impenetrable "sound barrier," and the loss of such a respected pilot was an ominous shock to the American high-speed researchers who felt that the

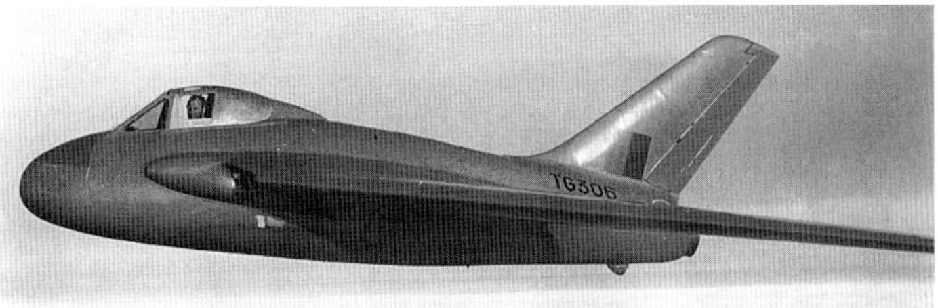

Geoffrey de Havilland peers at the *Flight* photographer from the cockpit of the second DH 108 Swallow prototype. On September 27, 1946, while flying over the Thames Estuary off Gravesend, in Kent, this aircraft entered a series of uncontrollable high-speed oscillations under compressibility at around Mach 0.88, causing the main spar to fail. The wings were ripped away from the airframe as a result of the disrupted airflow and the aircraft disintegrated, killing de Havilland. (*Flight*)

The US Navy's supersonic contender, the Douglas D-558-2, is seen here flanked by the Bell X-1E and X-1B in 1955. Restricted post-World War II funding severely limited the number of flights made by these research aircraft. (NASA Dryden Archive)

DH 108's low altitude and lack of an adjustable tailplane contributed to the accident. However, it was never a deterrent to their determination to pick up the supersonic challenge.

AMERICA ENGAGES

America had begun a concerted approach to producing a high-speed research aircraft in March 1944 when representatives of the US Navy Bureau of Aeronautics, the USAAF's Technical Service Command and NACA met at NACA Langley. Their discussions led in the end to separate initiatives by the USAAF, which followed Maj Ezra Kotcher's advice and eventually sponsored the rocket-powered Bell XS-1, while the US Navy and NACA began to work towards the less ambitious Douglas D-558-1 Skystreak based on specifications drawn up by US Marine Corps engineer 1Lt Abraham Hyatt and designed by Ed Heinemann. NACA was legally prevented from building its own research aircraft to avoid conflict with commercial manufacturers, so it had to rely on its influence, based on research data, on design choices and share a design with the USAAF or US Navy.

NACA's John Stack preferred an established power source to the more hazardous rocket alternative with its much shorter flight endurance, giving only two or three minutes of data collection. The D-558-1 was to be jet-powered by a General Electric/Allison TG-180/J35 engine – the first US axial-flow turbojet. It was also attractive to NACA and the US Navy because Douglas assured them that it could evolve into a combat aircraft. It had the same 18g load factor as the XS-1 and straight wings.

The High-Speed Panel, roughly the equivalent of the British Supersonic Committee, met in March 1944 and considered the lack of US data on supersonic research. Maj Kotcher, who had been project officer on MX-324 – the short-lived, jet-powered Northrop XP-79B Flying Wing – made far-reaching studies of rocket power. He was also a specialist in the study of aerodynamic flutter and vibration. The un-built XP-79 began as a rocket-powered design using an Aerojet Engineering Corps Rotojet 2,000lb-thrust engine powered by hazardous fuming nitric acid and mono-ethylaniline fuel. It had a blade-like wing that was to be used to ram enemy bombers, but it only flew as a scaled down prototype in July 1944. Nevertheless, it was the first US rocket airplane. A 6,000lb-thrust version was planned for the full-sized aircraft, but observations of the alarming ways in which its fuel reacted with metals like magnesium in the aircraft structure curtailed development.

However, Maj Kotcher concluded that rockets provided the extra thrust at high altitudes that contemporary, air-breathing turbojets could not generate for high-speed flight at the required altitudes. It also gave the chance of supersonic speed in level flight, where emergency recovery would be more possible than in a full-power dive. Rocket power did not require a drag-inducing air intake, simplifying the aerodynamic solutions compared with turbojet aircraft. In April 1944 the Wright Field Design Branch came up with its first proposals for a research aircraft – Project MX-524, the embryonic XS-1.

NACA's interest in supersonics had already been heightened in December 1943 by Robert Wolff from Bell Aircraft of Buffalo, New York, who attended a conference on jet propulsion in England. The latter convinced him that a Whittle-type turbojet could be used to power a supersonic aircraft. He expressed this view to Dr George Lewis, Director of Aeronautical Research at NACA, and received a positive response. Wolff had worked on the Bell XP-59A, and after his visit to the UK he was sure that far more powerful jet engines would soon be available.

Like the Miles team, Maj Kotcher's Wright Field researchers, including designers Capts F. D. Orazio and G. W. Bailey, found ballistics data the best guide for fuselage design. Maj Kotcher had attended Lt Col Zornig's lectures at Wright Field and he became convinced that the "sound barrier" was a compressibility phenomenon that occurred briefly at high subsonic speeds, but beyond that stable flight could resume. In the initial rough MX-524 sketches the bullet-shaped fuselage, with a flush canopy, supported a mid-mounted wing and a conventional tail unit. It housed a 6,000lb-thrust rocket engine,

The P-59 was America's first jet fighter, ordered from Bell on September 5, 1941 and powered by license-built Power Jets W.1 turbojets. Although it was armed and saw limited service with the 412th Fighter Group, it was an under-powered, big-winged craft that test pilot Pete Everest dismissed as little more than "just a powered glider." (USAF)

Lawrence Dale Bell, whose career in aviation began as a teenage mechanic for his brother's aircraft in 1912. He designed a rudimentary bomber for Francisco "Pancho" Villa, a prominent general in the Mexican Revolution, before joining the Glenn L. Martin Company, where he became factory manager and, in 1925, vice-president. He then spent ten years with Consolidated Aircraft Corporation prior to founding his own company in 1935 in Buffalo, New York, with Robert Woods. Bell Aircraft Corporation rapidly built a reputation for innovative designs. (Bell Aircraft Corporation)

based upon the regeneratively cooled 6000C-4 four-chamber motor that Reaction Motors Inc had been developing since 1941. The motor offered at least 2,000lb additional thrust compared with the General Electric/Allison TG-180/J35 turbojet.

In the absence of a suitable wind tunnel this basic configuration could only be proven through actual flight testing. Nevertheless, a contractor had to be found to build the MX-524, and in the summer of 1944 Theodore von Kármán asked Kotcher to find one. A chance visit to Kotcher's office by Robert Woods of Bell Aircraft on November 30 engendered Woods' enthusiasm for a project that had so far attracted no other bids. Woods had a particular interest in transonic flight, and Kotcher's assurance that the new aircraft would not, initially, be required to exceed Mach 0.8 persuaded him to commit Bell to engage in the project.

Woods, who had worked at NACA with John Stack, joined Bell from Consolidated, where he had engineered the A-11 ground attack aircraft. With Bell he designed the innovative P-39 Airacobra fighter, with its engine behind the pilot, and the FM-1 Airacuda bomber-interceptor that boasted two 37mm guns operated from turrets ahead of the rear-mounted engines. Wartime purchases of the P-39 pulled the company back from bankruptcy and production of the similar P-63 Kingcobra for the Soviet air force, together with sub-assemblies for heavy bombers during World War II, funded company research that led to the creation of the P-59A – America's first turbojet aircraft. The XP-59A contract had been issued to Bell on September 30, 1941 after Gen "Hap" Arnold had found out about the Whittle W.1 in April 1941 and arranged for the engine to be reverse-engineered by General Electric in the USA as the J31 or I-16. Woods' innovative skills also yielded the XP-77 lightweight fighter and XP-83 long-range jet escort fighter – neither design attained series production, however.

Having broken the news to a surprised Larry Bell, Woods began to work on the MX-524 outline based on his quick sketch that bore an astonishing resemblance to the eventual Model 44, or XS-1 design. He preferred turbojet power to Kotcher's rocket engine and substituted a General Electric J31 (a license-built Whittle W.1 at 1,650lb thrust), which was also used in the XP-59 Airacomet. With business prospects in mind, he also sketched in some guns for a jet-powered service version, but von Kármán wanted a research aircraft, not a fighter or a record-breaker.

The Wright Field Design Branch favored rockets and Woods' choice of powerplant was reversed when Kotcher showed him combat reports concerning the Me 163 rocket-driven fighter that had begun to harass USAAF bomber crews from mid-1944. This bat-winged, wooden fighter had reached an unofficial record speed of 622.6mph in level flight on October 2, 1941 after being air-towed to an altitude of 13,500ft. Armed with two 30mm cannon, the Me 163 was the climax of a series of German rocket-powered fighters that began with experiments by Fritz von Opel in 1928 using black powder pyrotechnics

At a conference to discuss the XS-1's supersonic flight are (from left to right), Joseph Vensel (head of NACA's Muroc flight operations), Gerald Truszynski (NACA instrumentation engineer), Chuck Yeager, Walter Williams (Head of NACA Muroc Flight Test Unit, with Bob Hoover's famous photo of 46-062), Jack Ridley and De Elroy Beeler (NACA X-1 project engineer). The small X-1 project team occupied primitive facilities at Muroc, a desert settlement whose first occupants in 1910 were Clifford and Ellie Corum. They had set up a small community that they christened after their surname, but in order to avoid confusion with Coram township in California, they reversed their name as "Muroc." (USAF Flight Test Center)

to power land vehicles at speeds up to 148mph – a development which one contemporary journalist described as "the first practical step towards the conquest of space."

Other rocket experiments in 1928 included a tailless, manned glider designed by Alexander Lippisch. Launched by rubber bands and then powered by rockets, this primitive and dangerous craft was the prototype for all subsequent delta-winged aircraft from the Me 163 to Concorde. Opel's assistant, Max Valier, outlined long-range vehicles powered by liquid propellant rockets while Opel planned large, passenger-carrying rocket-planes capable of 5,000mph. Opel's dreams were ended by the 1929 stock market crash and the death of Valier in an explosion the following year while experimenting with lox and alcohol – the fuel that would power the Bell XS-1.

The Me 163B was too late entering service and too difficult to fly effectively to have much more than a psychological effect on the unstoppable armadas of Boeing B-17 Flying Fortresses and Consolidated B-24 Liberators. Indeed, it probably accounted for fewer than 15 bombers, and accidents with its lethally corrosive hypergolic

The Me 163B was the first successful rocket-powered aircraft, and unlike the X-1, it was designed purely for military use. Despite its problems, the Me 163B showed that very short interception times were possible. For combat aircraft operating at medium altitudes, the rapid development of turbojets, using far less fuel and offering much greater endurance, became preferable to rockets, although the possibilities of combining the two powerplants were explored extensively. (USAF Museum)

fuel (hydrazine hydrate and methyl alcohol from distilled potatoes with a hydrogen peroxide oxidizer) caused many fatalities to its crews, despite their protective asbestos flying suits. However, its ability to climb six miles in three minutes and its 600mph speed – the fastest for any operational World War II fighter – in powered flights of 7.5 minutes had a profound effect upon US and British designers. The inherent dangers of its propellants certainly steered US designers towards less reactive, safer substances. Its comparatively thick wing also restrained it from supersonic speeds, confirming that a much thinner aerofoil was needed.

In America Robert H. Goddard (who would later design a turbo-pump system for the Bell XS-1's rocket fuel system based on a rocket system he built in 1940) had launched the first liquid propellant rocket, using petroleum and lox, in March 1926, and William Swan made an eight-minute flight in a rocket-powered aircraft in 1931. Liquid propellant rockets were already seen as a far more practical proposition than the hazardous solid-fuel alternatives.

Robert Truax, while serving in the US Navy during World War II, also devised a motor that had strong similarities to the unit that would power the XS-1. The rocket motor's simple Newtonian principle of

Resplendent in gloss orange (FS 12243) paint and World War II-style national insignia, the second XS-1 is dwarfed by its carrier B-29A, 45-21800. The end of World War II made the Superfortress, already Bell's favorite choice as carrier for the XS-1, available for peacetime uses. The Douglas C-54 Skymaster transport aircraft was another possibility, but it was also unavailable during the war years. (via Fred Johnsen)

equal and opposite reaction and its dependence on its own fuel rather than external air made it attractive for high-altitude flight in thin atmosphere. Simplicity of operation also meant light weight compared with jet turbines, as the motor was essentially a chamber where its fuel (such as alcohol and water) was mixed with an oxidizer, commonly lox, and combusted. It also required a pump system to propel the liquids into the combustion area and substantial, pressurized tanks to contain them. Usually, the pumps circulated the liquids around the exterior of the motor prior to combustion to provide cooling. Rockets were capable of far greater acceleration than contemporary turbojets, but their rate of fuel consumption usually limited burn time to just a few minutes.

In addition to Maj Kotcher's and Wright Field's preference for rocket power, the superior thrust-to-weight ratio and high-altitude performance of the rocket option were also pressed upon Robert Woods by his engineering staff. This included design engineer Benson Hamlin (a former flight test engineer on the B-17), stress analyst Stanley W. Smith, Roy Sandstrom (chief of preliminary design engineering) and project aerodynamicist Paul Emmons. Hamlin and Emmons also favored the "bullet fuselage" idea, although they acknowledged that most of their calculations would have to be based on estimates in the absence of hard test data. The team was led by Robert J. Stanley, Bell's exceptionally talented and hard-working chief of engineering and the company's former chief test pilot. He was also the first US jet pilot, having made the maiden flight of the XP-59A in October 1942.

Basic aerodynamic research into the MX-524 airframe continued throughout 1944. NACA Langley found that the air above a diving P-51D Mustang's laminar flow wing was actually travelling at Mach 1.2 when the fighter hit Mach 0.75. A P-51D was fitted with a small test model protruding from the gun compartment into the fast-moving airflow, and useful observations on various aerofoils were made in this "natural wind tunnel" environment.

By December 1944 the essential characteristics of MX-524 (later, MX-653) were decided. It was to be incredibly strong, being stressed to 18g, which was at least 50 percent more than any existing military design. This was mainly because the designers had no data to predict the kinds of aerodynamic loads that the aircraft would have to withstand, so caution and over-building were the guidelines for structural strength. Like the US Navy/NACA D-558-1, it had to carry 500lb of test instruments in a fuselage compartment and it would take off from a 7,000ft strip at 150mph. Benson Hamlin's initial design included a General Electric I-16 (J31) turbojet for initial takeoff and an Aerojet rocket motor for the high-altitude dash. The burden of two engines and their respective fuel supplies made for an overweight aircraft, so Hamlin replaced the J31 (which seemed unlikely to develop sufficient power anyway) with four jettisonable jet-assisted takeoff-type rockets. Crucial decisions were then made on the type of rocket propulsion and on the shape and aerofoil for the wing. Bell received a contract for three XS-1 (Experimental, Sonic, No. 1) aircraft on March 10, 1945.

CHAPTER THREE

THE SAFFRON BULLET

The wing center-section of the B-29A formed the bomb-bay ceiling in such a way that the X-1 had to be slung low, with only a few inches of ground clearance. The B-29A pilot also had to perform takeoffs with minimal rotation so that the X-1's tail remained clear of the runway, and made "flat" landings if the rocket-plane was still aboard. When launched, the sudden emergence of the X-1 from the darkness of the B-29's bomb-bay into bright sunlight briefly dazzled the rocket-riding pilots. Frost can be seen on the fuselage of the XS-1 in the liquid oxygen tank area as 46-063 and its "mother ship" taxi out for a mission from Muroc. (Bell Aircraft Corporation)

Selection of the correct wing profile, like several other aspects of the XS-1 design, was partly a matter of practical trial and guesswork. Without computers or high-speed wind tunnel results, the lack of information about the stresses that the airframe might face meant that the wing was built to withstand an unprecedented 18g. While the need for a thin aerofoil was generally agreed, it was not clear whether the ratio of wing thickness to chord should be ten percent (65,-110 aerofoil) or eight percent (65,-108) for the optimum combination of lift and low drag. It was not even known whether a workable eight percent wing could be built, as it was so much thinner than anything attempted previously for combat-type aircraft, which were usually up to 18 percent thickness/chord ratio.

Bell reckoned that an eight percent wing was feasible, although difficult, and it was used on the first XS-1 after initial flights with the slower ten percent version. NACA actually requested a 12 percent ratio initially, but Robert Gilruth of NACA, who at one stage insisted on a five percent wing, wanted a version that would take the aircraft further into the transonic range. He eventually accepted the USAAF's preferred ten percent figure.

There was general agreement that a small, thin, straight wing was desirable, partly because the USAAF wanted to study it in connection with its first operational jet fighter, the Lockheed P-80. This straight-winged single-seater originated as Gen "Hap" Arnold's platform for the British Halford H-1B turbojet. It first flew on January 8, 1944 after only 143 days between concept and building, and it introduced the USAAF to jet flying. However, more data was needed by Air Technical Service Command on how straight wings reacted at higher speeds for future P-80 development and next generation fighter projects like the Republic F-84 and Lockheed F-104.

The XS-1's 28ft span straight wing was also dictated by NACA's uncertainty concerning the behavior of swept wings across the speed range. Finally, it was almost certainly influenced by the choice of a thin, straight wing for the Miles M.52. Data from German aerospace engineer Adolf Busemann, director of the Braunschweig Laboratory and a pre-war swept-wing pioneer, and Robert Jones at NACA on wing sweep was encouraging, but there was a lack of test data to prove its efficacy at that stage. NACA, concerned about the security risks, was reluctant to pass on its German-originated data to the USAAF or aircraft manufacturers until late 1945.

Swept-wing models of the XS-1 were wind tunnel tested after the mock-up had been inspected in October 1945 and the lack of a swept wing had been commented upon. However, Hamlin's team, with advice from the USAAF's Air Technical Service Command, stayed with the straight wing, saving swept wings for the Bell X-2. The Douglas D-558-2, the US Navy contender for the supersonic role, was given a 35 degrees swept wing and 40 degrees swept tail partly because Douglas Aircraft designer Eugene Root had visited Germany to inspect captured research materials on swept wings in May 1945.

Manufacturing a straight wing that would withstand 18g required some innovative techniques. The upper and lower skins had to be milled from solid aluminum slabs to a half-inch thickness at the root, tapering to normal skin thickness at the tip. The thicker metal provided strength and also remained free of distortion in very turbulent transonic

Gen Henry H. "Hap" Arnold's long career in aviation spanned the period from the Wright brothers' earliest aircraft to jet fighters. Indeed, the USAAF's first operational jet fighter, the P-80, originated as his platform for the British Halford H-1B turbojet. Like the XS-1, the P-80 featured a straight wing. (USAF)

The three main sub-sections of XS-1 46-062 are lined up for final assembly in Bell's Buffalo factory in the late summer of 1945. Control runs and fuel plumbing lie above the rear section and the scientific instrument compartment above the extremely strong wing carry-through section is open. The airframe was subjected to thorough structural load testing before the final details were added. Test pilot Scott Crossfield described the XS-1 as a "model of simplicity." (Bell Aircraft Corporation)

airflow. For the eight percent version this gave a root thickness of just under 6in, allowing room for the 12 strain gauges and the lines to the 240 pressure measuring orifices that NACA installed in the left wing. Spoilers were mounted on the upper wing surface but their use tended to cause the nose to drop and a violent roll to commence at low speed. After the first 22 test flights they were fixed in the closed position.

There was general agreement with Robert Stack's proposal that the horizontal tail should have a different thickness/chord ratio to the wing so that it would encounter shockwaves at a different point in the transonic speed range, enabling control to be maintained. The eight percent wing was therefore paired with a six percent tail, while the ten percent wing had an eight percent tail, making that aircraft slightly slower. Gilruth suggested an all-moving tail, with conventional elevators for low-speed flight and movement of the entire unit to adjust its resistance to compressibility at transonic speeds. Essentially, as compressibility made the nose rise at high speeds and commence a pitch-up, the leading edge of the horizontal stabilizer (tailplane) was also raised slightly, forcing the nose down again.

A "butterfly" tail was considered for the second XS-1 but the final design used a horizontal stabilizer mounted on the vertical tail to avoid wake from the wing. Crucially, its angle of incidence was electrically adjustable by +/- 4.5 degrees from the cockpit to suit a range of subsonic and transonic speeds. This innovation was a key element in the aircraft's success, and it remained a secret throughout the XS-1 program.

None of the flying controls were power-boosted as it was felt that pilots would be able to cope with manual operation of such a small aircraft even in the demanding transonic region. However, a beefy H-shaped control yoke, which the pilot could grasp with both hands, replaced the conventional control column. Engine controls, stabilizer trim adjustment, a data-monitoring activating switch and other essential controls were located on it so the pilot could manage strenuous control situations without moving his hands from the yoke. In fact, pilots found the XS-1 was generally agile and light to control except in the most demanding areas of the speed envelope.

The narrow cockpit with an upward-sloping floor was designed to fit chief test pilot Jack Woolams, a "six-footer," sitting semi-reclined with his knees higher than his shoulders. It had a windscreen of double-layer laminated glass and methyl methacrylate, with a dehydrated space between them to reduce fogging. External straps were installed to add strength, although they obviously did little for the already minimal forward vision. For the third aircraft (46-064) a plate glass transparency was used, without straps, to withstand speeds up to Mach 1.6.

The cockpit was pressurized using nitrogen and a pilot's oxygen system was provided. Installation of an ejection seat was ruled out to save weight and because the prospect of high-speed ejection was considered too difficult at the time. Instead, the pilot had to fold away the bulky control yoke after pulling out a pin in its hinge, jettison

XS-1 CUTAWAY

1. Radio antenna
2. Elevator mass balance weights
3. Tailplane actuator sealing plate
4. All-moving tailplane
5. Tailplane electrical trim control mechanism
6. Elevator actuator motor and linkage
7. Snubber pads for suspension gear in B-29
8. Control rods and cable runs
9. Fuel filler pipe
10. Ethyl alcohol/water tank (made of stainless steel), 293 gallons
11. Spiral tube bundles containing nitrogen (two)
12. Wing carry-through structure and equipment "shelf"
13. Link points for suspension in B-29 launch bay
14. Fuselage access hatch
15. Liquid oxygen top-off filler point
16. Control rods and cable runs
17. Snubber pads for suspension gear in B-29
18. Double layer canopy with external bracing
19. Left side control console)
20. Pilot's control yoke
21. Airspeed/altitude recorder
22. Instrument panel
23. Spherical nitrogen tank (made of steel)
24. Pitot boom
25. Cockpit hatch (detachable)

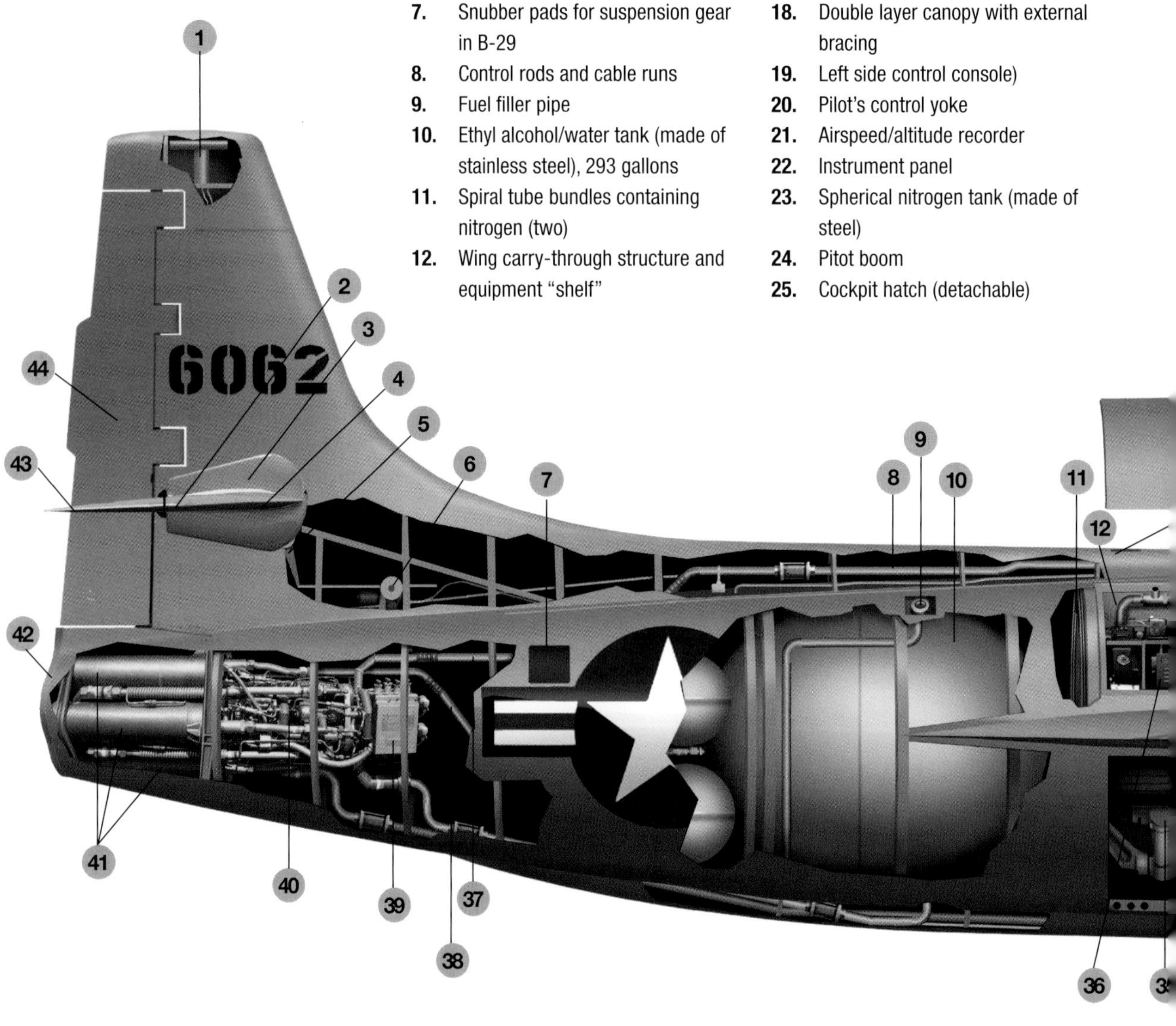

26. Rudder pedals
27. Battery
28. Pilot's seat
29. Oxygen cylinders, left and right sides
30. Nose landing gear (fitted with 16in × 5.8in tyre)
31. Liquid oxygen tank (made of steel), 311 gallons
32. Airspeed research sensor head
33. Spherical nitrogen tanks (made of steel – two)
34. Nitrogen supply for main landing gear strut
35. Main landing gear (fitted with 24in × 7.7in tyres)
36. Test equipment bay containing (typically) oscillograph, manometer, accelerometer and performance telemetry transmitter
37. Liquid oxygen feed pipe
38. Fuel (ethyl alcohol/water) feed pipe
39. Engine control box
40. Reaction Motors XLR11-RM-3 engine
41. Combustion chambers
42. Asbestos sealing plate around exhausts
43. Elevator
44. Rudder

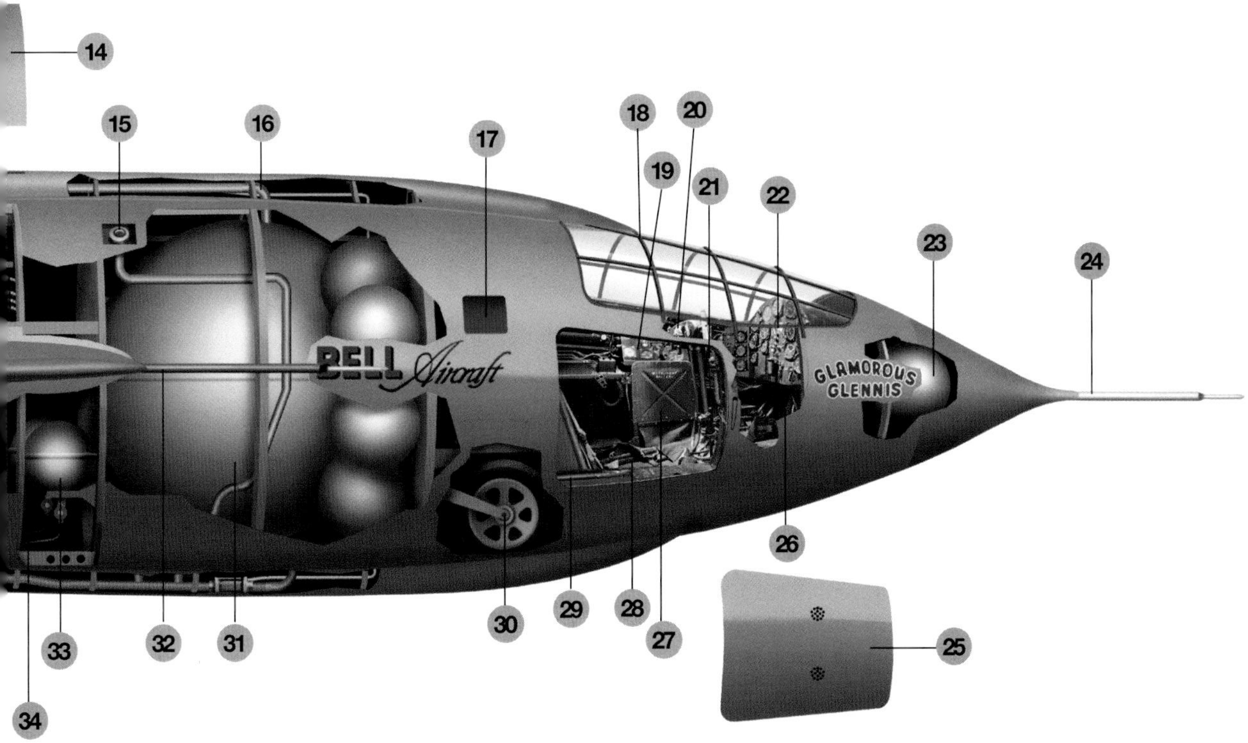

the cockpit side-hatch and bail out. All the pilots who flew the XS-1 were aware that the chances of hitting the sharp-edged wing or tail on exit were prohibitively high. Acknowledging this problem, test pilot Maj Frank K. "Pete" Everest still felt that, "If you lost control, or the airplane blew up or had a serious fire in the cockpit, then obviously you would try to get out of it. But that never occurred."

In Robert Woods' initial plans for the XS-1 as a design leading to a production combat aircraft, it would have taken off from the ground. Others at Bell, particularly Hamlin, believed that the airplane should be air-launched from a "mother" aircraft to give the longest high-altitude flight time with the limited available burn time of the rocket engine. The dangers of engine failure in the moments after takeoff, with a full load of hazardous propellants (particularly the hypergolic types) and no ejection seat were recognized by Robert Stanley and NACA. Hamlin therefore assumed that air-launching would only need a skid undercarriage, similar to the Me 163's, as a lightweight alternative to wheel units for landing. The final decision was in favor of air-launching but a retractable Bendix undercarriage was also installed, housed in the lower fuselage since the thin wing could not accommodate anything other than slender test-gear items. It was powered, like the flaps, by nitrogen to save the complication of separate hydraulics or batteries.

In other respects the airframe was relatively conventional in construction, but the rocket powerplant presented far greater challenges. Having rejected mixed turbojet and rocket combinations and the risky Aerojet 6,000lb-thrust hypergolic Rotojet, which used fumic nitric acid and aniline, the designers turned to the US Navy-sponsored 6,000lb-thrust rocket that was under development by the

ABOVE LEFT Preserved intact, the confined cockpit of 46-062 with its H-shaped control yoke, low seat position and raised rudder pedals. The altimeter gave measurements in 10,000ft increments up to 80,000ft, backed by another standard instrument that was accurate only up to 50,000ft. The Machmeter was also unreliable at high altitude, requiring Muroc's radars to provide accurate measurements of extreme speed and altitude. (National Air and Space Museum)

TOP The X-1's main flying instruments were confined to an altimeter, Machmeter, airspeed indicator, g-meter and an angle-of-attack indicator. Most of the other dials and switches related to the fuel system, radio and undercarriage controls. Herb Hoover insisted on changes to the cockpit of NACA's 46-063 before he would agree to fly it. These required three months of modification work, although they made for easier monitoring of some dials and valve operations. (National Air and Space Museum)

Reaction Motors Inc XLR-11-RM-3 Rocket Motor

1. Pressure switches
2. Main oxidizer valve
3. Nitrogen pressurization system pipes
4. Fuel (ethyl alcohol) pipes
5. Igniter chamber and spark plugs
6. Thrust chambers (four)
7. Fuel check valve
8. Binding strap
9. Exhaust nozzles (four)
10. Fuel connection
11. Evaporator coil
12. Oxidizer check valve
13. Electrical control feed
14. Main fuel valve
15. Propellant valve
16. Fuel (ethyl alcohol) inlet pipe
17. Oxidizer (liquid oxygen) inlet pipe
18. Thrust control box

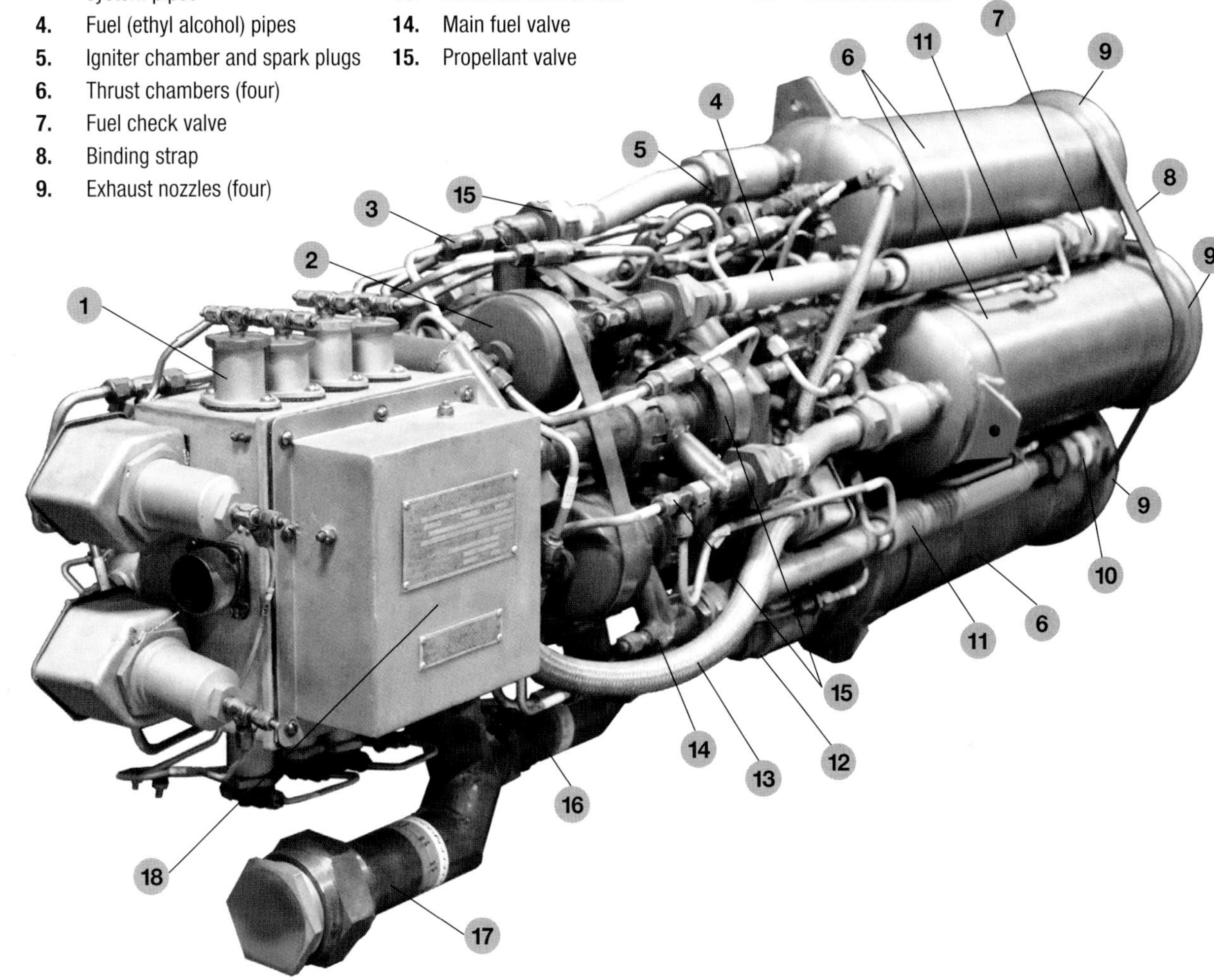

small Reaction Motors Inc (RMI) in a former nightclub in Pompton Plains, New Jersey. The company's James Wyld had previously worked with John Stack on aerofoils at NACA.

RMI were working on the 6,000lb-thrust XLR-8, weighing only 345lb, for the US Navy using four combustion chambers each developing 1,500lb thrust from non-toxic propellants that would not ignite spontaneously. It was completely American in origin, with no input from German data. Each cylinder had an igniter and a series of welded stainless steel tubes in which the much safer lox (burning at 127 gallons per minute) and mixed denatured alcohol/water propellant (five parts alcohol to one of water) were circulated in tubes around

RMI's outstanding, and noisy, XLR-11 rocket motor – this one is seen installed in the Martin Marietta X-24A lifting body. In its original LR-8 form, it powered the XS-1. (NASA Dryden Archive)

the combustion area prior to entering the chamber. This reduced the 5,000 degrees Fahrenheit internal temperature to around 140 degrees Fahrenheit on the motor's exterior.

The chambers could be used independently, and each one produced a quarter of the total 6,000lb thrust. Fuel was to be driven into the combustion chambers at 300psi by a turbine-driven pump supplied by Robert Goddard's company. RMI engineers gave Bell an ear-splitting demonstration of the black-painted prototype XLR-8 motor, which was later nicknamed "Black Betsy" and designated the XLR-11 in USAAF/NACA service. The motor had been adopted for the XS-1 by the time the USAAF issued its contract for the aircraft on March 10, 1945. The deal was done in the face of pessimistic forecasts of the XS-1's likely performance from NACA wind tunnel expert John Becker, who calculated that it would struggle to reach Mach 1.

Because there was some doubt concerning the availability of the Goddard turbine-driven pump in time for delivery of the engines for the XS-1's early flights, Bell fortuitously drew up a contingency system whereby the fuel system would be pressurized by nitrogen contained in 12 spherical steel tanks at 4,500psi. They were distributed within the circular cross-section of the fuselage wherever space could be found. Pressurization was achieved by the forcing of nitrogen through spiral tube bundles at the front and rear ends of the compartments for the spherical, steel lox and water/alcohol tanks, the nitrogen driving the lox/alcohol fuel into the rocket chambers.

The nitrogen pressurization system increased overall landing weight by 2,000lb, however, and drastically reduced the space for propellant from 8,160lb to 4,680lb. This in turn reduced the powered flight time by 50 percent to only 2.5 minutes. The pressurized propellant tanks were also inefficient users of space because their shapes could not follow the contours of the aluminum-skinned, semi-monocoque fuselage interior. Their sizes varied depending on the space into which they were to be installed. Also, the nitrogen supply had to be totally free of contamination from oil, water or other substances to avoid violent oxidation when it contacted the lox. It was understood that lox would also absorb the nitrogen, causing a reduction in gas pressure as the aircraft climbed to launch altitude. Pure nitrogen could not be obtained commercially in the required quantities and pressure so it had to be produced by boiling off liquid nitrogen in situ at the aircraft's fuelling area.

PASSENGER AIRPLANE

Ground takeoff would have ruled out a climb to 35,000ft or reaching much higher speeds than the P-80 could already hit in a shallow dive. One consequence of the reduction in anticipated performance was an indication from Wright Field that XS-1 tests should be flown from the vast dry lake "airfield" at Muroc, California, far from Bell's and NACA's usual east coast facilities. The company's P-59 jet fighter had been tested there in 1943, flown by Jack Woolams, who would make the first ten flights in the XS-1.

The main change resulting from turbo-pump delays was Bell's idea, outlined in September 1945, to abandon ground takeoff and launch the XS-1 from a B-29 "mother ship" at around 20,000ft. A B-29 had already been used to launch instrumented, lead-weighted missiles from

Groundcrew fill the lox and nitrogen tanks of X-1 46-064 with its revised, "strapless" cockpit canopy. The fuelling process was very time-consuming. The X-1's tanks fed the rocket motor through fuel lines at the base of each tank. Next to the lox nozzle is one of the thick canvas straps used to hoist the aircraft into the B-29A's bomb-bay for transportation to other locations. In a steep climb, with low fuel, it was necessary to keep positive g on the aircraft in a slight spiraling movement with the control column held back or else the fuel flowed to the rear of the tanks instead of flowing out into the fuel pipes, causing a premature engine shutdown. (NASA Dryden Archive)

30,000ft to study their behavior as they went supersonic. The XS-1 could then use its limited engine burn time to climb to 50,000ft and accelerate to at least 900mph. Although this was a drastic step, it was derived from earlier plans to air-drop large, unmanned test models or tow experimental manned aircraft to a launch altitude.

This idea also reopened the possibilities of flying from nearer locations such as Daytona Beach, Florida, or Marine Corps Air Station Cherry Point, North Carolina. Although this policy was initially resisted by NACA, B-29A Superfortress 45-21800 was supplied to Bell in October 1945 from World War II surplus stock for modification. NACA had to accept the air-launch principle, if only as a temporary measure while the turbo-pump was awaited. At that stage, when the aircraft had both its proven engine and turbo-pump, and might, therefore, take off from a runway, NACA stated that it would be ready to take over the XS-1. Another factor that tended to reduce NACA's influence over these decisions was a post-war reduction in its budget prompted partly by a sense that it had been slow to pick up on technological advances during the war, particularly those in Germany and the UK. As a result, the USAAF began to have a more dominant role in the XS-1's development.

This photograph of the X-1E being test-loaded beneath its B-29A carrier in 1955 shows how much of the bomber's structure was removed to accommodate the X-1. Pre-launch communications between the X-1 and Superfortress cockpit could present problems, as NACA pilot Robert Champine discovered. His radio failed and he wrote a message on his kneepad saying, "Secure the drop" (a US Navy expression meaning "stop") and passed it into the bomb-bay. The USAF crew were not familiar with the term and did not understand that he was cancelling the drop. Moments later he realized that he was actually about to be released and just managed to set up the X-1's controls in time as it plummeted down into the bright sunlight. A red warning light system was installed thereafter. (NASA Dryden Archive)

In November 1945, ahead of the completion of the first XS-1 the following month, a final decision was made by Bell and Wright Field that initial unpowered glide tests with the XS-1 should be conducted at Pinecastle Army Air Field (later Orlando International Airport) near Orlando, Florida. NACA, who by late October 1945 indicated that it wished to operate the aircraft after Bell's initial contractor flight testing, had insisted that the opening flight tests should happen at Langley Field. But Pinecastle had a 10,000ft runway, it was closer to Bell's headquarters and Wright Field, and its remote location in woodland amidst lakes and marshland would help to preserve the secrecy of the project. The US Army provided an optical tracker and SCR-584 radar unit to monitor the glide flights that would be made prior to the commencement of powered flights at Muroc. Wright Field provided a P-51H Mustang chase aircraft (replaced in February by a P-47N) and a B-17G photographic platform.

Fitting the air-launch carriage suspension devices added 60lb to the XS-1, but major structural modifications were needed for the B-29A. Its bomb-bay doors, gun turrets and main undercarriage doors were removed and sections of the lower fuselage close to the aft pressure bulkhead cut away to accommodate the XS-1's tail unit. The bomber's wing center-section passed through the fuselage, limiting its depth for carriage of the XS-1, and the available length of bomb-bay carriage space decided the length of the rocket aircraft's fuselage. The B-29A's rear fuselage allowed room for three observers. To restore stiffness to the aircraft's fuselage, steel beams some 40ft in length were installed along the bomb-bay. One D-4 bomb shackle was left in the bomb-bay to suspend the XS-1 and a sliding ladder was fitted into the bomb-bay wall so that the XS-1 pilot could climb down and enter his aircraft

through a hatch in the forward, right fuselage. The hatch door would then be lowered to him to be locked in place from the cockpit interior.

A release handle in the B-29 cockpit would drop the rocket aircraft, pushed away from the bomber's airflow by a compressed-air strut that exerted 3,000lb (reduced to 600lb after the first flight) to add to the estimated 1,500lb of aerodynamic down force on the XS-1 in its slightly nose-down position in the bomb-bay. In practice, two wooden guide rails were added to make sure the XS-1 fell away evenly without yaw or drift to the rear. A 6in length of steel tube protruded each side of the XS-1's fuselage to line up with the wooden guide rails. Both were coated with red paint to leave a mark on the XS-1 if it did move backwards or yaw on launching. After the first launch these guides were found to be unnecessary.

Before powered flights began six months later, a bomb-bay lox tank was installed to top up the XS-1's supply as it would boil off during the climb to altitude. A top-up nitrogen tank was also installed together with an extra catwalk and an emergency release lever to jettison the XS-1. The latter would have its uses later.

In mid-December the bomber was tested to 250mph at 30,000ft and several cameras were installed to film the launches. Loading the XS-1 into the B-29A's belly required a cross-shaped pit to be constructed into which the XS-1 was backed down a sloping ramp. The B-29A was then towed into position, along colored guidelines, above the smaller aircraft, and the XS-1 was winched up into position using two slings. Screw-jack sway braces tightened onto snubbers contacting the XS-1's upper fuselage sides to hold the orange rocket airplane steady.

XS-1 46-062 has been rolled backwards into the loading pit at Pinecastle AB and is waiting for its carrier B-29A to be maneuvered over it by a tow tractor. Similar pits were installed at Bell's Buffalo, New York, facility and at Muroc AB before the more versatile hydraulic lift system came into use at Buffalo and Edwards AFB. (Bell Aircraft Corporation)

As the first XS-1 (46-062) neared completion, delays began to occur with the supply of NACA's 500lb package of measuring instruments – a similar installation to the one placed in the D-558-2 Skyrocket. RMI was also having difficulties with the XLR-11. Explosions and fuel line surges occurred so that when the XS-1 had its first, unofficial roll-out at the Bell factory on December 12, 1945 it lacked an operational power source. Ground tests and modifications continued until the official roll-out on December 27, under ten months from contract signature. The first captive flight was made on January 10, 1946 to check the basic flight characteristics and use the XS-1's pressure monitoring system to study airflow over the wings and tail. Eight days later the "stork and baby" combination (depicted in nose-art on the B-29A) made the 4.5-hour flight to Pinecastle flown by Joe Cannon, with Jack Woolams aboard, ready to make the first test flights. The NACA delegation arrived the following day, headed by Walter C. Williams, with Norm Hayes in charge of NACA instrumentation in the XS-1.

At 1430hrs on 21 January Harold Dow flew the B-29A off Pinecastle's runway with the XS-1 clutched in its belly for the first captive flight. It was a dry run rehearsal for the first glide flight, which was delayed until January 25 while further adjustments were made to the XS-1's controls and better weather was awaited.

When Dow and Joe Cannon reached the correct altitude in the B-29A on January 25, Woolams squeezed through the bomber's forward crew compartment hatch onto a narrow bomb-bay walkway. From there he mounted the flimsy crew ladder, shielded on its forward side from the 200mph windblast. He then had to bounce on the ladder, hanging more than 5,000ft above open space, to make it extend parallel to the XS-1's open cockpit hatch. With further contortions he worked his way into the cockpit in the semi-darkness and connected his straps, oxygen, parachute and headphones. Crew chief Mac Hamilton, poised on the ladder, then lowered the weighty cockpit hatch into position on chains, before turning around on the ladder to push the door into position with his backside. Then Woolams operated the lock with his right hand. It was a challenging procedure that would be successfully carried out on 50 occasions prior to the first supersonic flight taking place.

Woolams then discovered that the door had not formed an airtight seal and, worse, no heat from the B-29 was being pumped into the icy-cold cockpit during the slow, spiral ascent above Rosamund Lake. Cabin sealing problems persisted throughout the XS-1 program. He endured this as the bomber climbed to 25,000ft, where its inboard Wright R-3350 engines were feathered and its flaps lowered to 25 degrees, setting a launch speed of 180mph. On later flights the flaps were set to shallower angles. After a countdown from "ten," Dow pulled the bomb-shackle release and the XS-1 fell away evenly, exactly as planned. Jack Woolams allowed it to accelerate to 275mph, finding it pleasant and light on the controls, "delightful to fly" and commendable for its "ruggedness, noiselessness [freedom from aerodynamic turbulence when gliding] and smoothness of response." He checked undercarriage and flap operation and stall characteristics.

The "stork and baby" nose-art that adorned B-29A 45-21800 was applied during the early stages of the high-speed test program. The bomber was supplied to Bell in October 1945 from surplus war stock. (via Fred Johnsen)

Jack Woolams

Born on February 14, 1917, and with a ranching and rodeo-riding background, Jack Woolams joined Bell Aircraft's experimental research department in 1941 following 18 months of service with the USAAC's 79th Pursuit Squadron. He subsequently became the first man to cross America in a fighter when he flew a P-39 non-stop from Los Angeles to Washington, D.C. in 11 hours. In 1943 Woolams flight-tested the XP-59, America's first jet aircraft, setting a new unofficial altitude record of 47,600ft, after a previous flight in which he reached 45,765ft without a pressurized cockpit or heating. In a high-speed dive test his YP-59A lost its tail and he had to kick the jammed cockpit canopy off in order to escape.

Woolams was appointed chief test pilot for Bell in 1944. While he was performing the first XS-1 flight tests he and fellow Bell pilot Alvin "Tex" Johnston indulged their love of air racing by modifying two war-surplus P-39 Airacobras for the prestigious 1946 Thompson Trophy air race. Renowned North American Aviation pilot George "Wheaties" Welch, Bell's "Slick" Goodlin and Lockheed's Tony LeVier were among other company test pilot participants. On a pre-race, low altitude test flight over Lake Ontario on 30 August 1946 Woolams' windscreen probably collapsed at speeds in excess of 400mph, decapitating the pilot as his P-39 plunged into the lake. Johnston, who had tried to resign from the company when Larry Bell told him not to take part in the race, went on to win the Thompson Trophy.

Jack Woolams demonstrates the awkward access to the cockpit of the orange-painted second XS-1, the first to fly from Muroc in October 1946. Crew chief Jack Russell (left) worked on many landmark test aviation events ranging from the first American jet flight by the XP-59A, through the X-1 programs to the entire series of flights by the X-15. (Bell Aircraft Corporation)

Jack Woolams had been certain that he would make the first supersonic flight in the XS-1, and so was the USAAF. His mixture of consummate flying skills, calm professionalism and wild off-duty antics confirmed his legacy as a pilot who certainly had what came to be known as "the right stuff."

Approaching the runway towards the end of his ten-minute flight, Woolams dived quite steeply through scattered cloud to improve his restricted view through the windscreen and landed on a grass overrun some 400ft short of the runway (which was obscured by trees) at 105mph without damage. Later that day Woolams celebrated by inviting the Bell crew to a nearby rodeo, where he demonstrated his skill in riding a bull!

Nine more glide flights followed at Pinecastle through February, with pauses for B-29 maintenance, separation of the XS-1's landing gear and flaps control operation and adjustments to NACA's instrumentation. Unpowered speed passed 400mph in a dive, and up to three flights per day were scheduled, although poor weather interfered with this plan. Otherwise, all went well until the fourth "drop" when the left landing gear started to retract during the landing run. At 80mph the left wingtip contacted the runway, but Woolams managed to hold the small craft fairly steady until its wing encountered a sturdy runway border light. The damage was slight but the XS-1 had to be returned by B-29 to the Bell factory for two weeks of repair, delaying further flights until February 19. On that day the nose wheel retracted prematurely, fortunately towards the

Boeing (Renton)-built B-29A-96-BW 45-21800 bears an XS-1 aloft. The rocket-plane's frosted belly indicates a fully topped-off oxygen tank and its open hatch is ready for the crew entry ladder to be lowered. Despite occasional engine problems, the B-29A provided reliable service as a carrier. Its US Navy equivalent P2B-1S Superfortress, used for the parallel D-558-2 Skyrocket program, avoided a gruesome disaster for pilot Jack McKay when its runaway No. 4 engine shed a propeller. His Skyrocket was dropped seconds before the whirling prop scythed into the Boeing's bomb-bay rocket-plane housing, severing some control cables. Co-pilot, X-1 pilot and future astronaut Neil Armstrong brought the bomber home safely on three engines and half a control system. (Bell Aircraft Corporation)

end of the landing run, requiring minor repairs and alterations to the extension mechanism.

Handling as a glider proved to be exceptionally good and trouble-free throughout nine flights, although on the ninth Woolams had to cope with another phenomenon that would recur. As he entered the landing pattern the windscreen de-icing system deposited its glycol on the canopy, making it opaque. Just as he was contemplating the possibility of jettisoning the cabin door to give at least sideways visibility to attempt a landing, the glycol venting stopped and vision was restored just before touchdown.

For this final Pinecastle flight on March 6, ballast was added in the fuel tank spaces to give a more realistic idea of the XS-1's behavior at weights approaching those with the engines and some fuel in place. At the conclusion of another successful flight word was received that Bell wanted the aircraft back at its factory for a personal inspection by Maj Gen Benjamin Chidlaw, deputy commander at Wright Field. The ten flights had shown that the basic air-launch process and the XS-1 itself had met all the requirements. The move to powered flight could proceed with confidence.

CHAPTER FOUR

RIDING THE ROCKET

While the Pinecastle tests proceeded, Bell worked to fulfill the rest of its contract with the remaining two first-generation XS-1s. They also re-fitted an eight percent wing structure and six percent tailplane to the first aircraft and an evaporator for the high-pressure nitrogen system that was needed pending the long-delayed delivery of the Goddard/General Electric turbo-pump.

Both new XS-1s, 46-063 (completed for NACA in June 1946 with the nitrogen system and thicker wing) and 46-064, were externally similar to 46-062 but 46-064 was expected to use the turbo-pump. Bell tested a prototype turbo-pump throughout December 1946 but it failed persistently. However, deletion of the nitrogen spheres in 46-064 enabled internal fuel storage space to be considerably increased to 437 gallons of lox and 498 gallons of diluted ethyl alcohol. A small tank with 31 gallons of hydrogen peroxide was added to power the turbo-pump. In April 1946 46-062 was at Buffalo being equipped with nitrogen, fuel tanks and modified flying surfaces for its powered debut. Bell received the first fully tested XLR-11 rocket motor on March 23 and a second engine, received in July, was run extensively in a test cell at the company's Niagara Falls facility. There were two cases of rocket chamber burnout.

With the completion of the initial Pinecastle phase of contractor testing it became clear that the USAAF was keen to take the lead from NACA, led by Walt Williams, in pushing ahead with management of the powered flight stage once Bell had completed its acceptance trials. The latter required it to demonstrate powered flight up to Mach 0.8 and controllability up to 8g. NACA, at the same time, was fighting to

Black crosses were painted on 46-063 to assist with photo interpretation. It also has a pitch and yaw vane assembly under its nose boom for its early flight trials. The design of the three pressure regulators for the X-1's nitrogen system took considerable effort, and refining them occupied many hours during the flight test program. They were all controllable from the cockpit. One reduced the initial pressure from 4,500psi to 1,500psi and the other two took the pressure down to 340psi for each propellant tank. They could be closed to let the propellant tanks depressurize. The nitrogen spheres were thought to be good for up to 800 "fills" before they would explode. (NASA Dryden Archive)

NACA XS-1's program at Muroc was led by engineer-in-charge Walter C. Williams, who supervised the activities of several research projects at the site between September 1946 and July 1954. (NASA Dryden Archive)

fund new projects including a supersonic wind tunnel. It saw this as part of the venture that included the XS-1 with the turbo-pump driven propellant system, taking off from the ground, together with overall supervision of the XS-1 program.

For Bell, which was already suffering post-war scaling down and financial problems, the XS-1 project was increasingly important to the company, which wanted to see it achieve its goals rather faster than NACA seemed to require. Bob Stanley and NACA's senior XS-1 leader, Walter Williams, often clashed. Williams asserted that NACA pilots could not be risked in an aircraft that had undergone, "such limited acceptance tests as Bell proposes." Financially, it was now in Bell's interests to accelerate the test program because so many other firms were fielding innovative designs with spectacular speed and altitude performances at the secret Muroc desert airfield. When the XS-1 finally arrived there were already 31 other prototypes being tested.

DESERT DEBUT

The move to the inhospitable Muroc Army Air Field was inconvenient for both NACA and Bell, but it was the only base large and remote enough for the next stage of the XS-1 program. It offered good weather (although the temperatures could rise to 115 degrees Fahrenheit), and the vast 65 square miles area of Rogers Dry Lake – the largest in the world – was available for emergency landings. Its clay surface could support up to 250psi and it was smoothed over every winter when it briefly flooded and the cracks in the clay were filled in. Muroc had been an Army site since 1933, and it offered basic military facilities. Nevertheless, living conditions were primitive, there were frequent sandstorms and rattlesnakes were abundant.

Woolams and Bell had previous experiences of the place, and in anticipation of his series of powered flights, the former, who had suggested the move to Muroc, took charge of establishing the Bell operation, complete with fuelling facilities for the XS-1 and accommodation for the team in the available "Rat Hotel" barracks.

A NACA team was also assembled and an SCR-584 radar unit was obtained to track the XS-1 flights. Less welcome for NACA (even than the primitive conditions) was the fusillade of Press coverage, fuelled by Wright Field, for Jack Woolams and his forthcoming flights in which he would allegedly "risk certain death to break the sound barrier, achieve speeds of 1,500mph at 75,000ft and open the doors to interplanetary travel." NACA was alarmed by these exaggerated claims, and by the lack of credit for its own part in the venture. Its personnel were already annoyed at their accommodation, in which they had to shake the wind-blown sand out of their bed sheets every night.

Jack Woolams had taken on other tasks during the six-month hiatus after Pinecastle, including early work on the Bell X-2 and the swept-wing Bell XP-63N (or L-39), but his fatal crash on August 30, 1946 during a test flight for the Thompson Trophy Race threw all plans into

Chalmers H. Goodlin

Jack Woolams' replacement was destined to receive almost as much Press coverage, although his popularity was more limited. Chalmers Goodlin, who was born in Greensburg, Pennsylvania, on January 2, 1923, became obsessed with motorcycles and aircraft from an early age. Indeed, he made his first solo flight at 16. Inspired by the RAF's performance in the Battle of Britain, Goodlin abandoned his intended farming career and enlisted in the Royal Canadian Air Force (RCAF). In training he earned his "Slick" nickname for accurate instrument flying. The youngest officer in the RCAF at the time of his commissioning, Goodlin was posted to the UK in mid-1942 and eventually joined a Spitfire squadron. Transferring to the US Navy in December 1942, he performed acceptance tests for new aircraft until released from service in late 1943.

Bell employed Goodlin as a test pilot in January 1944, and he was lucky to escape from burning aircraft on two separate occasions. Like Chuck Yeager, his lack of a college degree was outweighed by his intuitive piloting skills. Larry Bell gave him the XS-1 pilot role in September 1946 when he was only 23. He left the program after 26 XS-1 flights and joined the embryonic Israeli Air Force (IAF) at the suggestion of a Hollywood friend. Flying a Spitfire IX, he was involved in a dogfight in which three RAF Spitfires were shot down due to misidentification during the 1948 Arab-Israeli War. Goodlin subsequently became chief IAF test pilot and, flying a DC-4, transported thousands of Jewish refugees to Israel. He later formed airlines in the Seychelles and Holland and finished his career as CEO of the Burnelli Company, specializing in aircraft designs with wide, aerofoil-shaped fuselages. Goodlin was furious at his unsympathetic portrayal in the 1983 film *The Right Stuff*, based on Tom Wolfe's book.

Chalmers "Slick" Goodlin in the cramped XS-1 cockpit. (Bell Aircraft Corporation)

confusion and shocked Larry Bell, who had been close to Woolams. Rather than passing the XS-1 role to "Tex" Johnston, however, Bell selected a younger company pilot, Chalmers Goodlin, as pilot and made Johnston the program supervisor.

After a practice captive flight from Niagara Falls on September 26 the B-29/XS-1 combination departed on the ten-hour flight to Muroc on October 7. The first glide flight, with 46-063 aboard, was delayed until October 9 while full NACA instrumentation was awaited. Goodlin entered the XS-1 at 7,000ft but the cabin pressure began to increase to dangerous levels once the nitrogen pressurization system was activated. His only option was to jettison the cabin door once it had its lowering chains re-fitted. The door was released with explosive force that dented it as it hit the entry ladder, bending the ladder away from the aircraft and rendering it inaccessible for escape. The cockpit pressure instantly fell to a safe level.

Unable to return to the safety of the B-29's cockpit, Goodlin elected to sit out the return and landing in the suspended, doorless XS-1 with a good view of the gaping void inches from his seat. The door was later straightened with a sledgehammer, the ladder was repaired and the mishap was traced to a misplaced rubber gasket in the cockpit pressurization lines. The project flirted with disaster on numerous occasions due to faults such as this, caused by seemingly small, insignificant components.

Goodlin, like Bell's autocratic Robert Stanley, was interested in reaching the contracted speed target of Mach 0.80 as soon as possible, and he found NACA's slow and methodical progression by stages irksome. NACA wanted a strict progression with a set number of maneuvers at each speed increment before moving up the next fraction of a Mach number. Flights would carry increasing loads of water in the fuel tanks to prove the propellant jettisoning system and assess the aircraft's behavior when air-dropped at increasing weights. On the first attempt the tanks were inadvertently filled with contaminated water, requiring time-consuming disassembly and flushing of the complete system. The USAAF also bridled at NACA's imposition of such a rigid, measured program.

Testing experienced delays due to the slow delivery of spare parts, many of them hand-made for this unique aircraft, and by unexpected storms at Muroc. Goodlin did not make his first glide flight until October 11, when cockpit pressurization was a problem again and the brakes failed on landing, requiring a landing run of more than 7,000ft on the dry lake. This and the next "drop" (when the brakes failed again) were ideal opportunities for him to confirm the aircraft's excellent, if slightly over-sensitive, handling qualities at diving speeds up to Mach 0.71. Unfortunately NACA's data collection was limited to a few seconds as their short-run recording package had been turned on too early. It was agreed at this time that Bell would make 20 flights in all and then pass 46-063 over to NACA, which would provide its own pilot – possibly Goodlin on a new contract, although he appeared far less enthusiastic about the XS-1 than Woolams had been.

It was December 2 before another jettison test flight could be made, using water/alcohol tank ballast. The fuel jettison system worked well, venting 1,930lb of water/alcohol, although the XS-1's release shackle had to be operated manually by crew chief Mac Hamilton, perched inside the bomb-bay. Proving that the fuel could be dumped was crucial because the XS-1 would be unable to land safely unless all of its fuel had been burned off or vented. The last portion of the propellant load was always jettisoned to prevent the motor from overheating when the fuel, also used for cooling, ran out.

POWER ON

An attempted powered flight four days later was aborted when frozen valves in the nitrogen system meant that the system could not be pressurized to start the motor or jettison the propellants. Then the nose wheel suddenly extended. As the rocket airplane's ground clearance was normally less than 1ft, this meant that the B-29 could not land safely with the XS-1, with its undercarriage extended, still aboard. Luckily, Goodlin was able to retract the nose wheel partially just before landing.

The first powered flight was then planned after more static tests of the rocket motor. Unexpected problems continued when the tanks were filled with real fuel. For example, hydraulic fluid froze in the wheel brake lines where they passed very close to the lox tank. However, it was unexpectedly bad weather that caused the flight to be abandoned after takeoff, and it was re-scheduled for December 9 after further modifications to the nitrogen system. Although there were still nitrogen pressurization difficulties prior to the "drop," it was made successfully at 27,000ft and Goodlin noticed how the fuel load, increasing overall weight to 12,012lb, accelerated the fall away from the B-29A and made the XS-1 tail-heavy. After ten seconds he triggered one chamber of the XLR-11 and felt the aircraft accelerate powerfully as he briefly lit the second at 35,000ft.

The XS-1's admirable stability and internal quietness impressed Goodlin, as did the aircraft's rapid rate of climb and acceleration to Mach 0.795, almost hitting the maximum allowable Mach 0.80 with only one chamber burning at any time. He skillfully controlled some loss of directional stability caused by fuel sloshing around in the tanks and jettisoned some of it to maintain the correct fuel tank pressure. As the aircraft descended to 15,000ft he lit all four chambers and was pressed hard against his seat as the XS-1 roared upwards in a steep climb towards 40,000ft, leaving the FP-80 chase-plane far behind. In the ascent Goodlin was concerned that the fuel mixture was incorrect, indicated by a drop in lox pressure and a howling sound. He shut down the motor. Seconds later his attention was caught by a red fire-warning light. The P-51 chase-plane of project engineer Dick Frost eventually caught up with the meteoric XS-1, at which point Frost detected smoke briefly streaming from its tail. Goodlin was able to land safely at the end of a generally successful first powered flight.

In the wake of his exploits on December 9, the Press began to portray Goodlin as a fitting replacement for Woolams in euphoric articles written about the flight. Indeed, they compared him to Columbus, Magellan and the Wright brothers! Despite it being a supposedly secret program, the XS-1 project seemed to be providing the Press with plenty of material, much of it reported inaccurately. However, for cash-strapped Bell, the unsubstantiated rumors that the XS-1 would become a fighter was welcome publicity, and NACA was relieved to have its role in the program given some exposure.

A NACA technician prepares data-recording equipment for the instrument bay of the second XS-1. Installing and calibrating the various instrument packages of telemetry transmitters, oscillographs, manometers and accelerometers took up a considerable amount of time between flights. (NASA Dryden Archive)

The flash fire on December 9 had caused damage to the XS-1's wiring around the engine and charred some NACA instruments, requiring modifications. Stainless steel tubing replaced aluminum alloy in the motor, ram-air scoops were installed in the rear fuselage and asbestos liners were wrapped around the rocket cylinders. The rocket ignition sequence was revised to avoid sudden ignition or shutdown of all four chambers simultaneously, preventing sudden over-pressure and fuel line fractures. The fire was later attributed to a loose igniter allowing fuel to briefly spray onto its hot surface, bursting some nitrogen pipes. It could have been much worse.

Flights resumed on December 20, but there were persistent problems with the nitrogen pressurization, in one case because the lox tank at minus 296 degrees Fahrenheit cooled the nitrogen too much for it to activate the propellant valves. Lox was situated behind the cockpit, which made the pilot's conditions cold but bearable if the cockpit heating system worked. NACA data was not recorded on that flight as Goodlin forgot to switch on the instruments, leaving Williams' two female "computers" with nothing to analyze that day.

The aircraft was grounded until January 6, 1947 while further modifications were made to the engine and fuel regulators. On January 8, despite the recurrent cabin pressure issue and low chamber pressure problems inhibiting ignition, Goodlin achieved Mach 0.795 and some useful NACA data was recorded. The January 17 flight included a brief but unintentional dash at Mach 0.828 – over the preset speed limit – without incident, despite some tail buffeting that prompted the removal of the ram-air scoops. They were later replaced when it was shown that they did not cause the buffeting.

The next two flights were aborted after more in-flight fuel pressure difficulties, but four successful launches were made from January 22 to 31, with an FP-80 Shooting Star chase-plane replacing the Mustang. Following every flight there were minor recurrent problems with igniters, tank pressure and brake failure, but Bell and NACA worked relentlessly to perfect all aspects of the aircraft in preparation for the next phase of the program in the face of more budget cuts. Between flights the aircraft often had to be virtually disassembled to check all the safety valves, diaphragms and seals in the complex pipework for the fuel and nitrogen supplies. The engine was pre-fired before each flight and then the tanks were re-filled, taking many hours for each three-minute powered flight in a 15-minute sortie.

In February Goodlin flew more calibrated runs at various speeds and made high-g pull-ups. He also explored the XS-1's tendency to roll to the left at speeds near the stall. Finally, there was time for him to be fitted with a pressure suit for higher-altitude flights. Tests with 46-063 continued until February 21, and these threw up irritating snags such as tiny debris in a lox regulator, which curtailed one flight.

With 46-062 due to complete its modification program – it was being fitted with a thinner eight percent wing structure and six percent tailplane – in March, 46-063 was airlifted back to Niagara Falls by B-29 on February 28. Here, its propulsion system would be modified and improvements made to the stabilizer controls as requested by NACA for its own forthcoming research program. Joel Baker and Mel Gough at NACA Langley still had reservations about the nitrogen pressure system, the pilot's visibility and the stabilizer controls, but nothing could be done to change these basic design features at that time with more funding cuts looming. There had already been criticism of the cockpit layout, non-adjustable rudder pedals and poor windshield defrosting. Wright Field personnel, on the other hand, were concerned that during the comparatively lengthy XS-1 test period the aviation industry had begun to test jet-powered, swept-wing combat aircraft that would probably demonstrate performance figures that were not much below those anticipated for the XS-1.

The "saffron bullet" existed partly to prove that supersonic flight was possible, but time was pressing and both the USAAF and Bell (particularly Robert Stanley) still wanted results faster than the cautious NACA approach seemed able to provide them. By March, Larry Bell and Stanley had begun talks that implied a continuation of Bell's participation in the costly program and a re-emphasis on using the XS-1 to make the first supersonic flights. A program of up to 60 flights was suggested by Dick Frost, taking the third (turbo-pump) XS-1 all the way to Mach 2. The USAAF's interest was duly aroused and further discussions lay ahead to shift the program back towards Bell and the military. By April 1947 Air Materiel Command, aware of shrinking funds, had decided to take over the supersonic project and make those flights as soon as possible with minimal NACA instrumentation. As compensation NACA was offered the second XS-1 for its sole purposes.

46-062 returned to Muroc on April 5 and "Slick" Goodlin made ten more flights in it up to June 5, 1947. An initial glide flight on April 10 with the tailplane in the neutral trim position showed a tail-heavy tendency which required a re-setting of two degrees "up" to bring the nose down. The aircraft's new wing gave it a slightly larger turning circle but otherwise its handling characteristics had hardly changed. The first powered flight took place the next day and it ended in a nose-wheel collapse on landing.

Repairs took until April 29 and flights resumed with a slightly increased drop speed from the B-29. Goodlin explored pull-ups and stalls at various speeds and altitudes. He also experimented with adjustments to the tailplane, increasing the angle from one degree to 2.5 degrees as speed increased from Mach 0.55 to 0.75. The pressurization system's relief valves continued to present difficulties, causing two aborted flights on May 1 and 5, but Bell still expected to complete its part of the program by the 23rd of that month. A flight was attempted on May 15 but Goodlin found that the ailerons were very stiff, possibly due to frozen moisture in the damping system. There were also leaks in the nitrogen pipes. Several more flights were made but pressurization difficulties still persisted. With only four more flights left in the program (two in each XS-1) Goodlin made what would be

Chuck Yeager being interviewed with XS-1 46-062 in the Muroc fuelling area. The title on its nose indicates the take-over of the XS-1 program by the Army Air Force Air Materiel Command's Flight Test Division in May 1947. (USAF Flight Test Center)

his last in 46-062 on May 21. It was a glide flight from 30,000ft that tested the airframe to 8g in pull-up maneuvers. He then had to land with his windscreen almost totally iced over by frozen breath escaping from the dehydration cylinder attached to his oxygen mask.

XS-1 46-063 was returned to Muroc on May 8 to begin NACA's work, with Joel Baker assigned to fly it. However, he resigned in mid-May after a disagreement and there was no one else ready to replace him. While NACA sought to organize its program, Col Boyd at Wright Field's Flight Test Division proposed a new plan that would enable Bell to make another 30 graduated flights with 46-062, leading to attempts at a new world altitude record and speeds up to Mach 1.1. Bell would work to a fixed-price contract and the USAAF would provide a test pilot at a cheaper rate than Bell had to pay its pilots. Bell rejected the offer and the USAAF looked to NACA instead as partners in a transonic program using both XS-1s. The third XS-1 (46-064), with an eight percent wing and six percent tailplane, was put on hold, pending funds. NACA became unenthusiastic about such cooperation and about the XS-1 generally and did not relish the idea of the fast-track program that was proposed. However, it agreed to continue in a joint venture with the USAAF.

CAST CHANGES

NACA's revived XS-1 46-063 was ready for its first test flight on May 22, and in the absence of a NACA pilot Bell's "Tex" Johnston was scheduled to take it. Johnston, who had initially been briefed on the XS-1 by Jack Woolams back in March 1946, was impressed by its flying qualities but found the rudder and tailplane control slow to react and the motor ignition slightly unreliable. He looked forward to further exploration with the airplane, but it was to be his only flight in it. Goodlin's last trip took place a few days later to investigate buffet boundaries. On this May 29 flight he too found the tailplane trim control operation too slow.

The first two XS-1s and their "mother ship" B-29A at Muroc AB on June 18, 1947. Bell's contractor flights had been completed in the previous month and USAF flight trials were initiated on July 27, although the first flight was not made until August 6. (USAF)

Goodlin made a final, brief demonstration flight for the Aviation Writers' Association on June 5. On this occasion in 46-063, Goodlin made a spectacular dive and high-speed pass at 7,000ft, igniting two chambers as he passed over the crowd. He then gave a noisy ground-based demonstration of its rocket engine that actually ended with an internal engine fire. This was the last flight for the XS-1 for two months, as fire damage to 46-063 was so severe that Bell replaced its entire rear fuselage with parts from the uncompleted third aircraft.

Goodlin had assumed that he would be pilot for continuation flights by Bell and the USAAF, including the supersonic dash. A handshake agreement between himself and Stanley in

September 1946 considerably enlarged the normal $10,000 bonus for completing the company acceptance tests. Indeed, it gave Goodlin another $150,000 for taking the XS-1 through to supersonic speed and beyond, paid over five years by the USAAF within their contract with Bell. The larger sum was in recognition of the risks involved in the supersonic phase, but no firm contract was drawn up to cement the deal. The impending loss of XS-1 leadership to the USAAF and NACA made the bonus payment more difficult for Bell, and the firm's lawyers advised Goodlin in June 1947 that the company could not now make a commitment to it. Goodlin met with Stanley on June 10, and when he saw that the decision was final he immediately resigned.

Goodlin had always fulfilled the terms of his contract, although many among the Muroc team regretted that he never went beyond his role as pilot to become more involved with the engineering and planning issues of the program, as Woolams had done and Yeager would do. His tendency to spend his free time (of which there was a great deal due to all the delays) off-base in Hollywood with friends did not endear him to the team either.

These circumstances made it easier for Bell and the USAAF to see Goodlin go, and to seek a cheaper solution, but it was also one that put the Air Force in the driving seat for the project and Bell out of it after more than three years of invaluable foundation-building. The company had proven the aircraft and its power system in 37 test flights, 19 by Woolams and Goodlin in the first XS-1 and 18 by Goodlin and Johnston in the second. Of these, 23 had been rocket-powered and the propulsion system was seen to be generally reliable and less hazardous than many had forecast. XS-1s had reached Mach 0.82 and coped with loads of 8.7g.

The company was, in any case, looking ahead to its swept-wing, Mach 2 X-2 aircraft by this time. But Col Boyd was very keen to see a USAAF test pilot involved in such a prestigious program as the XS-1. The formation of the USAF as a separate entity from the Army on July 26, 1947 created a need for public recognition in what was now a three-way battle for the defense dollar and consequently greater inter-service rivalry with the US Navy, which was pressing ahead with its rival D-558-2 Skyrocket for the supersonic prize. All were impelled by the overwhelming belief in the power of technology to confirm America's newfound superiority in defense engineering post-World War II. Dr Hugh Dryden, NACA's new Director of Research from September 1, 1947, was a noted proponent of transonic flight research. Col Boyd, dubbed "the father of USAF test pilots," working in an air force that had not funded its own test pilots for more than 20 years, also saw the value of the XS-1 project, redesignated X-1 after July 1947. He saw it creating a new image for the new USAF, using service pilots who would be prepared to take on the challenge. All he had to do was find the right candidate, and he had a clear idea who that should be.

Chuck Yeager beginning the awkward process of easing into the XS-1's cockpit. An XS-1 pilot had to trust the aluminum ladder as he slid it downwards parallel to the cockpit aperture, battered by the B-29's 220mph slipstream and the unprotected thunder of its four Wright R-3350 Duplex-Cyclone turbo supercharged radial engines. When parallel with the square cockpit opening, he had to slide in, legs first, and strap in before putting on a flying helmet that would almost touch the canopy. (USAF/AFFTC)

CHAPTER FIVE

"POKING THROUGH JELLO"

The success of the X-1 project depended on the "carrier aircraft" principle, using a Boeing B-29 or B-50 to haul the aircraft up to an altitude where its limited rocket-powered endurance could be used most advantageously. The X-1's open cockpit hatch can be seen in this dramatic takeoff photograph. (via Fred Johnsen)

Chuck Yeager was among the many P-51 Mustang pilots who experienced compressibility and bone-jarring buffeting when diving his aircraft in combat during World War II. He met it again post-war as Assistant Maintenance Officer at Wright Field, service testing the Bell XP-59A, Lockheed XP-80 and Republic XP-84 Thunderjet among many other types. These experiences all confirmed him as a pilot with great intuitive skills and a sound understanding of engineering, acquired during his years as an aircraft mechanic. His cool, level-headed reputation recommended him to Col Boyd, who replaced Lt Col Counsel as head of the Wright Field Flight Test Division. Counsel had already favored Bob Hoover as designated pilot for the USAF's X-1 test program, but the uncompromising Albert Boyd decided that Hoover's inverted buzzing of Springfield Airport in a P-80 jet (a Federal Aviation Authority safety violation) indicated a lack of what he saw as the "right stuff."

Hoover's undoubted ability still qualified him for the back-up and chase pilot roles, but Yeager became the Colonel's first choice for the rocket ride after Maj Kenneth Chilstrom presented him with a list of Wright Field test pilots who were interested in the project. He did express reservations when he discovered that Yeager was married. He had not wished to expose a family to the risks inherent in the project, and he also had Gus Lundquist as another possibility until he was ruled out by a depth perception problem with his vision. Boyd was aware that the X-1 had already demonstrated buffeting and instability problems and "is liable to go in any direction, or all of them at once." Yeager would find these words prophetic in due course, but he was up for the challenge.

Capt Chuck Yeager with Maj Gustav Lundquist and Capt Jim Fitzgerald, who performed stability and control investigative flights in *GLAMOROUS GLENNIS* in 1947. On Lundquist's June 3, 1948 flight to Mach 0.98 the left main undercarriage door flew open, causing a difficult trim situation. The nose wheel also collapsed on landing. (Bell Aircraft Corporation)

Despite his disappointment, Hoover remained good friends with his fellow pilot and both men entered a punishing course of tests in a centrifuge, a high-altitude pressure chamber and cumbersome David Clark pressure suits in preparation for the test flights. They visited the Bell factory and watched a frog being immersed in lox and then broken apart when dropped on the floor. They were shown the X-1, which Larry Bell told them was indestructible, looked thoughtfully at the "escape" hatch and the fatally sharp wing edge and then sat in the cockpit while the XLR-11 was cranked up to a brain-numbing shriek.

Robert A. Champine and Herbert Hoover with the second X-1, identifiable by the single set of pressurization vent holes in the hatch door. 46-062, by contrast, had two sets. Champine had previously been a US Navy fighter-bomber pilot, and he initially tested Bell's L-39, which was a P-39 Airacobra with swept wings that "Slick" Goodlin also flew for the Bell X-2 program. Bob Champine was then checked out in the X-1 by Herb Hoover, before making 12 further flights in the aircraft. (NASA Dryden Archive)

Hoover might well have recalled his conversations with captured German scientists concerning one Luftwaffe pilot who was literally dissolved by propellants when his Me 163 overturned on landing. In a cancelled project, an Me 163 had been scheduled for test flights at Wright Field post-war, and Hoover was to have been the test pilot. No doubt it occurred to the two intrepid aviators that they would be undertaking this hazardous occupation on standard Air Force captain's pay of $283 per month, rather than the $150,000 bonus that Goodlin was rumored to have demanded. Col Boyd had even squashed suggestions of a $25,000 bonus for the first supersonic pilot, saying "the Air Force will do it."

Boyd selected an outstanding team to run the project and gave them relative freedom to operate at Muroc, with supervision by him from Wright Field. Overall management also rested with James H. Voyles, civilian X-1 project engineer, and Paul F. Bikle, chief of Air Materiel Command's Flight Test Division Performance Engineering Branch. Finally, Capt Jack Ridley, who knew Yeager well, was given the job of program manager and engineer-in-charge – a position that paralleled the role of Walt Williams for NACA. He was well qualified for this demanding job, possessing exceptional engineering skill and a calm approach to solving technical problems. Capt Ridley had gained a master's degree at California Institute of Technology, studying under Theodore von Kármán – the long-established proponent of supersonic flight. Ridley's expertise was seen in the development of the variable incidence tailplane that enabled the X-1 to cope with transonic compressibility.

Bob Hoover was a World War II Spitfire pilot with the USAAF's 52nd Fighter Group (FG) who had become a prisoner of war after being shot down on his 59th mission off the coast of southern France in early 1944. Like Capt Ridley, he was recommended to Col Boyd by Yeager. Hoover later flew many types as a test pilot and had a long-standing reputation as an aerobatic and stunt pilot, although he would never have a chance to fly the X-1. Jack Russell, Bell's crew chief for the X-1, was hired by the USAF in the same capacity. Dick Frost, who had worked on the X-1 since the origins of the design, was seconded from Bell as project engineer and passed on his intimate knowledge of the rocket airplane to Jack Ridley, Yeager and Russell. He also flew many of the chase sorties for flights by the X-1 series and later became test pilot for the Stanley Company's ejection seats for many US fighter types.

The USAF officially took over the X-1 on July 10, 1947, and also had to crew the attendant B-29A. Mexican-born Maj Roberto Cardenas, formerly director of Wright Field's Experimental Engineering Laboratory flight test unit, was chosen as pilot. He had previously flown B-24 Liberators until he was shot down in March 1944. Like Yeager, he had been able to evade capture and was eventually returned to the USA as a test pilot. Cardenas flew the P-59, Northrop YB-49 Flying Wing and other prototypes. Not only would he pilot the faithful B-29A, with Lt Ed Swindell as flight engineer, he would also act as administration officer for the X-1 project.

The team that set up shop at Muroc on July 27, 1947 included six USAF personnel and 15 carried over from Bell. NACA remained closely involved in data monitoring, with around 12 personnel at Muroc. The project, however, usually required around 30 NACA people overall – roughly a tenth of the number subsequently employed for the hypersonic North American X-15.

NACA's Muroc Flight test unit was established under Walter Williams in August, and its two aviators, Herbert H. Hoover and ex-US Navy pilot Howard C. Lilly, were indoctrinated in X-1 technology by Dick Frost. The three-way program-sharing continued to work effectively, although there were tensions between NACA and the USAF over the pacing of the flight schedule. Wright Field's enthusiasm to attain the supersonic prize before the US Navy had to be combined with NACA's more measured progression towards the collection of sufficient research data. It was also known that North American Aviation was intending to use its new XP-86, first flown on October 1, 1947, to attempt supersonic flight with a production jet fighter.

Yeager completed ground school on the X-1 on August 1, 1947, ready to perform his first unpowered flight on August 6. On the latter date he was dropped by Cardenas at 18,000ft and pursued by Bob Hoover and Dick Frost in P-80s. Yeager broke with established protocol by doing three slow rolls during his descent. To some, this was evidence of a pilot with excessive testosterone, but Yeager saw it as a way of becoming familiar with the X-1 and demonstrating the ease of handling which he immediately discovered in it. He made two more unpowered flights, indulging in a mock dogfight with Hoover's P-80 on the second on August 8. The X-1 was in many ways at its most maneuverable without fuel, as "Pete" Everest later discovered. "It was a nice little airplane and very easy to fly except when it was loaded with propellants. It became sloppy then." He attributed this partly to the fuel's weight and its tendency to slosh around in the tanks. "Once the propellants were halfway gone the X-1 flew like a decent airplane. When they were completely used it flew more like a glider."

Chuck Yeager with his distinctive helmet, parachute and the XS-1's nickname, which its subject, Mrs Glennis Faye Yeager, said was airbrushed out of photographs taken at the time of the first supersonic flight. The nickname was repainted in at least two styles. The black rectangle to Yeager's left is a contact patch for the stabilizing "snubber" that kept the X-1s steady while in place within the B-29 or B-50 bomb-bay. (NASA)

The launch procedure was by then well established. The pilot had to make his way from the B-29A cockpit to the bomb-bay catwalk and descend the extending ladder, squeezing himself into the cockpit. In Yeager's case this was a slightly easier task than it had been for the taller Woolams. Once the door had been lowered with Ridley's assistance and locked from the inside, the pilot then worked through the extensive pre-flight checklist. A few minutes before launch he initiated ("dome-loaded") the first-stage gas regulator, followed by pressurization of the lox and alcohol/water tanks. They would reach the designated pressure just before launch, allowing the pilot to squirt propellant from the airplane via the emergency jettison system so that the chase pilot could check that the latter was indeed functioning. At the correct altitude (usually around 21,000ft) Cardenas gave a countdown from ten, with the word "drop" usually being followed by a pull on the B-29A's cockpit handle that opened the bomb shackles to release the X-1.

ACROSS THE BARRIER

Capt Yeager's first powered flight occurred on August 29, with the X-1's nose bearing the name *GLAMOROUS GLENNIS*, after his wife. Variations on this name (including *GLAMOROUS GLEN III*) had appeared on his wartime P-51Ds. Dropped at 21,000ft and 255mph, he noticed the more rapid descent due to the extra weight of loaded fuel tanks. At 500ft below the "mother ship" he ignited all four rocket chambers individually, finding that chamber No. 3 temporarily shut down when he performed another slow roll (to Frost's astonishment) due to a drop in lox pressure with zero g. Under strict instructions to stay below Mach 0.80, Yeager put 46-062 into a steep dive and hit Mach 0.84 as he leveled out below 2,500ft and progressively ignited all four rocket chambers in a climb over the Muroc base. He increased the climb angle to 45 degrees, but the aircraft still accelerated to Mach 0.85 before the motor was shut down. Yeager completed his exhilarating ride by making a series of stalls before landing.

NACA's hopes of useful data from the flight were dashed when it was discovered that the telemetry and cockpit camera equipment had not operated successfully. NACA personnel were also unimpressed by Yeager's deviations from the flight plan. He had already shown some impatience with Walt Williams' strict scientific schedule for each flight. Although a terse disciplinary response from safety-conscious Col Boyd was expected when he heard of Yeager's excessive speed, the errant pilot was merely, but strongly, reminded that neither he nor the airplane was expendable, and that a steady progression towards the higher speeds was mandated. Yeager promised to behave.

The flight was repeated on September 4, when Yeager made a level speed run at Mach 0.84 and 30,000ft. He found the X-1 to be stable, with no buffeting or need for trim change from the selected stabilizer setting of two degrees down. It quickly reached Mach 0.865 (later recalculated as Mach 0.89) with two chambers burning, and

Capt Yeager, photographed by Jack Ridley, demonstrates the semi-reclining position necessitated by the XS-1's bullet-shaped nose. Although this posture helped with resistance to g (as later F-16 pilots learned), it did little to enhance the pilot's minimal forward vision. However, pilots who were used to landing piston-engined fighters like the P-51 were used to limited forward visibility. Yeager later re-enacted this famous scene at the National Air and Space Museum to mark the 50th anniversary of his first supersonic flight. (USAF Flight Test Center)

accelerated stalls at Mach 0.80 were then induced, with little indication of any more than mild buffeting. A soaring climb to 41,000ft burned off the rest of the usable fuel. The X-1 was proving to be a lively but extremely manageable aircraft which seemed to present no unexpected problems. Sadly, the NACA data was partly unrecorded once again, although the X-1's highest speed could clearly offer information that exceeded the available wind tunnel results, which were only valid up to Mach 0.85.

Yeager made three further flights, with a telemetry failure once again on the first, to capture the elusive data, reaching Mach 0.92 at 36,200ft on September 10. NACA engineers (who believed that Yeager had forgotten to switch on their data pack on at least one of the flights) noted a nose-up trim change at Mach 0.88, and a tendency for the nose to "tuck under" at Mach 0.92 – something that Yeager had not considered serious. The fifth powered flight, on September 12, went well, yielding full data at speeds up to Mach 0.925, but before Yeager could push further into the upper transonic range he had to return to Wright Field to be fitted with a partial pressure suit for altitudes above 50,000ft, where the ultimate speed runs would be made.

Yeager's first task upon returning to Muroc was to make the acceptance flights for the second (NACA's) X-1 on September 25, as he was the only pilot qualified to do so. NACA had installed four new instrument panels, improved its fire prevention measures and revised the flap actuators. Some nose wheel and instrument parts had to be borrowed from 46-062 to replace those damaged in 46-063, delaying the USAF program. It also had a series of persistent leaks in its fuel-line pipe work that held up its flight program. The first X-1 was restored to flight status by the end of September, a new tailplane actuator motor having by then been installed to give a faster rate of trim change at three degrees per second. It was October 3 before flying could resume, Yeager testing the new actuator at speeds up to Mach 0.88. At this point a pronounced Dutch roll and right-wing heaviness were noticed, as had been the case on some previous flights. Yeager thought this was caused by fuel sloshing around in the tanks.

The gradual speed increases continued, with Mach 0.945 chalked up on October 8 (the 48th flight in the program) and Mach 0.997 two days later in a flight that ended in a zoom climb to 45,000ft. At that altitude thick frost formed inside the cockpit canopy and Yeager could not scrape it off. Denied external vision and reliant on the

X-1's only "blind flying" instrument – an attitude gyro – he had to be talked down by Dick Frost in his attendant P-80 jet. Data analysis showed that Yeager might already have exceeded Mach 1 on that flight, but in any case it was clear that the official "barrier-breaking" flight was only a step away.

This momentous occasion was scheduled for October 14, but the final push was almost jeopardized by another type of barrier that did not break. At the end of a night celebrating at the Muroc crews' favorite venue, Pancho Barnes' "Rancho Oro Verde Fly Inn Dude Ranch" (a bar where, as US Navy test pilot Bill Bridgeman put it, "neither the language nor the glasses were very clean") on Sunday October 12, Yeager and his wife decided to take a horseback ride across the moonlit desert. On return it was too dark to see that someone had shut the gate to the corral and Yeager's galloping horse struck the gatepost, throwing its rider to the ground. In great pain, but not wanting to miss his crucial flight, he surreptitiously visited a doctor in nearby Rosamund and found that he had two broken ribs. Strapped up with tapes, he was returned to Muroc by Glennis that afternoon and confided his situation to Jack Ridley. Bob Cardenas was also aware of the injury and trusted Yeager's judgment, but others including Dick Frost only found out about it much later.

The X-1's nitrogen system was already being pressurized and there was no time to seek further remedies, apart from one. Yeager told Ridley that his injury prevented him from making the awkward movement needed to lock the cockpit door with his right hand. The ever-resourceful Ridley found a broom handle and cut off a ten-inch

Bob Hoover's historic shot of Chuck Yeager passing his FP-80 chase-plane on October 14, 1947. He could see Yeager approaching from behind him and had his camera ready as the X-1 streaked past with shock waves in its rocket exhaust. Understandably, this is one of the few air-to-air photos of a first-generation X-1 at speed. The dark streaks above the left wing were caused by oil leaking from the B-29A's engines while the X-1 was suspended in its bomb-bay. President Truman received a copy of this picture the following morning. (USAF Flight Test Center)

length for Yeager, who could use it in his left hand to lever apart the two rods that locked the rollers on the door. A few practice runs in the cockpit showed that it was possible, so the stick was placed in readiness. Another homespun solution was also crucial. Crew chief Jack Russell, who had joked with Yeager about his fall but was unaware of the broken ribs, coated the canopy interior with Drene shampoo as an anti-icing agent.

Yeager climbed aboard the B-29A and at the appropriate time he managed to make his painful way down the ladder and into the X-1's cockpit. He strapped in, locked the door with the broom handle lever and went through his check list, setting the tailplane to one degree nose-down as the B-29 spiraled up into a gin-clear sky to the 20,000ft drop altitude. Falling away into the dazzling sunlight Yeager lit the four cylinders in sequence (but forgot to turn on the NACA data-collection pack for three minutes) and then climbed at Mach 0.88 on two chambers, aiming for Bob Hoover's white contrail. He re-adjusted the "flying tail" tailplane to two degrees nose up, ascended to 35,000ft on all four cylinders and hit 42,000ft travelling at Mach 0.92 – the speed at which the NACA specialists had warned him to exercise particular caution before accelerating further. With a third of his fuel still left Yeager re-ignited chamber No. 3 and noticed mild buffeting as he passed Mach 0.93. However, this eased as he accelerated. "The faster I got, the smoother the ride," he reported.

Elevator effectiveness was restored at Mach 0.96, as Yeager had predicted. He pressed on to Mach 0.98, the fastest speed by any human at that time, and felt acceleration suddenly increase. His Machmeter needle flickered as the shockwaves rolled back across the airspeed sensors and then "tipped off the scale. I thought I was seeing things! We were flying supersonic, and it was as smooth as a baby's bottom." He sustained the speed for another 20 seconds and then raised the nose to slow down, famously reporting to Ridley that "there's something wrong with this Mach meter. It's gone screwy."

There was momentary turbulence as the X-1 decelerated through Mach 0.98 and Yeager jettisoned the remaining fuel and began his descent, performing some victory rolls and aerobatics on the way home. At Muroc, the distinctive double-crack of Yeager's supersonic boom was both evidence of their success and the starting pistol shot for a new era of supersonic flight. Yeager's 14-minute sonic excursion, which he downplayed as "poking through Jello," had actually topped out at Mach 1.06 (700mph). The news was passed back to Wright Field and a celebration at Pancho's was quickly planned, but cancelled when Col Boyd informed the Muroc team that the flight was to be kept strictly classified.

Private parties were arranged instead at the Yeagers' and Frosts' homes, culminating in a high-speed motorcycle ride without headlights as Yeager's means of returning home. Anaesthetized by martinis, he survived a crash en route and continued his journey in total darkness, outdistancing Frost's car. For the man whom

The second X-1 with one of the nose-probe sensor configurations used in 1950. NACA pilot John Griffith, who joined the team in September 1949, is in the cockpit and handing his helmet to groundcrewman Dick Payne. Team members Ed Edwards, holding the entry hatch door, and Clyde Bailey are also present. Griffith achieved the fastest speed for this aircraft, Mach 1.20 on May 26, 1950, and also flew the Douglas D-558-1 and -2. (NASA Dryden Archive)

Gen Hoyt Vandenberg (USAF Chief of Staff) once described as "that damned hillbilly," it had been a long, painful day that seemed to end almost with official denial of his achievement. Fortunately, there were plenty of government luminaries who wanted to acknowledge his achievement and he was taken to Washington, D.C. to be awarded the Distinguished Flying Cross (DFC). His self-effacing honesty won over the top brass and those who were jealous of his success, but Boyd had decreed that there was to be no promotion or profit from his achievement. He remained a captain for another seven years, and he and Glennis continued to live in sub-standard accommodation at Muroc while the X-1 program entered its next stage.

BEYOND THE BARRIER

Yeager flew the X-1 seven more times, four of them in October and most of them at supersonic speeds. On November 6 he reached Mach 1.35 (890mph) at 48,600ft, far beyond the semi-mythical sound barrier, and on March 26, 1948 he reached Mach 1.45 (957mph) – the fastest speed attained by an X-1. The emphasis then passed to the NACA effort, with Herbert Hoover's first powered flight on December 16 in 46-063 reaching Mach 0.71 and incrementally advancing to Mach 0.925 by the end of January 1948. Hoover was seriously injured while testing a Republic P-84 and he was replaced in the NACA team by Capt James Fitzgerald (later killed in a September 1948 TF-80 crash), but Hoover returned to the X-1 and made the first supersonic flight by a civilian pilot on March 10, 1948, followed by Howard Lilly on March 31. Lilly was killed while testing the second Douglas D-558-1 in May 1948, and he was replaced by Robert Champine.

The two X-1s went on to make a total of 158 flights by October 1951, including two piloted by Jack Ridley and one supersonic sortie by Col Boyd himself. Yeager's achievement had energized and speeded up the program, including NACA's approach to it, while also improving collaboration between the participants in the project. It also brought some extra funding to improve living conditions at Muroc. The small-scale Research Airplane Program, initiated mainly by John Stack in 1944, was becoming an integral part of the development of aviation in the USA. Scott Crossfield, who in November 1953 would fly the

US Navy's D-558-2 Skyrocket at 1,291mph and become the world's first Mach 2 pilot, joined the X-1 team in April 1951 and made ten flights. He too suffered a windshield icing incident but managed to clear a small area with his sock and Ridley talked him down to a safe landing. The persistent problems of nose-wheel failure, occasional engine fires and pressurization difficulties continued to cause delays, but much was achieved nevertheless.

Chuck Yeager, Jack Ridley and *GLAMOROUS GLENNIS*. The bottom edge of the pilot's extending ladder is seen near Ridley's shoulder, giving some sense of the perilous nature of this cockpit entry method when used at 7,000ft altitude. Its lower edge was tapered to match the X-1's fuselage contours. Ridley excelled as a pilot, as an engineer and as a teacher of complex aeronautical technology to aircrew, fellow engineers and mechanics. Yeager and the X-1 team relied heavily on his intuitive ways of solving problems. (USAF Flight Test Center)

NACA's 46-063 remained in use until October 1951, flown by John Griffith, Scott Crossfield and Robert Champine from the newly named NACA High-Speed Flight Research Station at Muroc. The latter had in turn been re-named Edwards AFB in January 1950 to honor Capt Glen Edwards, killed in a Northrop Flying Wing accident northwest of the base on June 5, 1948. NACA's X-1 was used primarily to measure aerodynamic loads, stability and control at high speeds.

NACA flight 54 was made on October 23, 1951, with Joe Walker aboard. The aim was to investigate buffeting using wing vortex generators, but the engine cut out and Walker had to glide home. Inspection of the airframe showed leaking battery acid and impending structural failure of the nitrogen spheres, so 46-063, painted white during its October 1948 repair period, was permanently grounded. It would reappear in white in 1955, but completely rebuilt as the sole X-1E.

The security clampdown on Yeager's flight began to weaken in December 1947 when initial data on the program was prepared for use by the aviation industry. The magazine *Aviation Week* obtained and disclosed basic details of the supersonic flight in its December 22 edition, triggering potential prosecution by the Attorney General via the FBI. Crucially, no mention was made of the all-moving tail innovation, one of the main reasons for the secrecy.

The USAF delayed confirmation of the supersonic flight for six more months, announcing at a ceremony on June 15, 1948 that three USAF pilots and two from NACA had broken the "sound barrier" on numerous occasions. Yeager was publicly commended and awarded another oak leaf cluster for his DFC and the Mackay Trophy for the most meritorious flight of 1947. Another ceremony was held on December 17, 1948, where Yeager, Stack and Larry Bell were awarded the Collier Trophy for the greatest achievement in aviation for 1947. Yeager allegedly kept the handsome trophy in his garage for a while as a container for spare nuts and bolts. The delay in announcing the supersonic flight yielded one advantage in that information about the "flying tail" also remained classified, allowing time for it to be incorporated into the design of many planned combat aircraft.

Yeager's first flight after the October 14, 1947 record was a potential disaster. Scheduled to reach Mach 1.08 on October 27, he was released by the B-29A and immediately discovered that his battery switch was inoperative (due to a tiny amount of corrosion on one of the terminals) so the X-1 had no electrical power. Crucially, he could neither power up the engine nor jettison his three tons of fuel, ruling out an attempted landing. Yeager prepared for a bail-out, knowing that it would probably be fatal, but then recalled that the ever-resourceful Jack Ridley had anticipated just such an emergency and installed a valve with a separate bottle of nitrogen gas to force the fuel out of the system. With this as his last hope Yeager began to expel his 604 gallons of fuel as the dead-weight X-1 plummeted to 10,000ft. With no radio contact, he had to assume that the jettison process was working. He then commenced an approach, lowering his undercarriage without an indicator to show whether the landing gear units were indeed locked down, and alighted safely.

The November 3 flight was aborted when the X-1 could not be released because a safety pin had been left in one of the bomb release shackles, leaving the airplane suspended a few inches below the bomb-bay but impossible to drop. There was no choice except to land with it in place after jettisoning the fuel, but Yeager scrambled back up into the B-29 for that event. Fortunately, there was still enough ground clearance for Cardenas to pull off a "flat" landing without scraping the X-1. When exactly the same thing happened on Yeager's next flight he started to un-strap ready to leave the cockpit when the X-1 suddenly broke free and fell away in a near-stalled condition. He managed to regain control after a 5,000ft fall and ignited the rockets to complete the flight. Incredibly, there was a third flight with the same problem the following day, and on that occasion Yeager watched in awe as a courageous, parachute-wearing sergeant stood on top of the suspended X-1's fuselage, whacking the jammed shackle with a sledgehammer.

On three high-altitude supersonic flights in January 1948 Yeager was alarmed to notice smoke in the cockpit. There were also small fires in the engine compartment. Flying far above his chase pilots, who could have advised him about the severity of the fires, he was unable to do anything but dump fuel and hope that the fire would not spread. Several more flights were terminated by fire-warning lights in the following weeks. Neither Russell nor Ridley could find any faults in the engine, but Yeager began to have terrifying nightmares and said that he "felt like a condemned man." Bell established that the engine had incorrect gaskets installed during an overhaul, causing the overheating, but Yeager was ready for a break from the X-1 and had plenty of other test work to carry out on other prototypes.

However, there was one more crucial flight to come. Increasingly annoyed at the US Navy's jibes at the X-1 as a supersonic "cheat"

X-1 46-063 baking in the sun on the flat, dry Muroc surface in 1949. The small bulge on the nose cone covered two lines from the static pitot boom that had to curve around the nitrogen sphere housed in the nose. (NASA Dryden Archive)

because it was air-launched, unlike their D-558-1, the USAF asked Yeager to demonstrate the X-1 with a ground takeoff. Yeager had also upset naval top brass by upstaging their D-558-1 Skystreak during a public display of the US Navy's rival aircraft with a near-sonic pass close to the viewing stands in his F-86 chase-plane as Skystreak pilot Gene May made his demonstration run. Ridley was concerned that the X-1's weak undercarriage might collapse on takeoff under the weight of fuel, but he eventually decided that the demonstration was feasible.

On January 5, 1949 Ridley and Yeager carefully calculated a half-load of fuel and the exact time it would take the oxygen to boil off. Yeager lit all four rockets, took off at 200mph after a 1,500ft ground run and soared to 23,000ft at Mach 1.03 80 seconds later. The incredible acceleration snapped the undercarriage actuating handle and blew off the wing flaps, but the aircraft landed safely after the first (and probably only) such takeoff by a rocket-powered airplane. Yeager reckoned that, to the USAF, he was "a bigger hero for beating the Navy to the punch than for breaking the sound barrier." The publicity surrounding Yeager's flight also greatly enhanced the ethos of the service test pilot in the USA.

The second Skyrocket was converted for air-launched flights from a B-29A in January 1951 after its turbojet engine was replaced by an LRM-8-RM-2 rocket motor similar to the X-1's, and it made a supersonic air-launched flight on November 17, 1950. The third D-558-2 (BuNo 37975) used both jet and rocket power and achieved supersonic speed from a ground takeoff on June 24, 1949.

Maj Frank K. "Pete" Everest, another World War II fighter ace with extensive experience, checked out in the X-1 on March 21, 1949. At that time Col Boyd planned a change of emphasis for the final stage of the X-1 program, prioritizing high-altitude flights rather than pushing for higher Mach numbers. Everest was asked to explore aircraft behavior above 50,000ft, where blood would boil if the cockpit pressurization failed. His second flight on March 25 was supersonic, but curtailed by a damaging engine fire. The following flight was to have been a high-altitude attempt, but only two rocket chambers would light and severe pressure on Everest's eardrums, exacerbated by a head cold, ruptured an ear-drum.

He carried a spare helmet for use instead of the pressure helmet when his continuing ear pain recurred, but on one flight he accidentally re-connected the helmet's oxygen tube to the nitrogen exhaust outlet. As a result he almost blacked out and lost control of the aircraft. A last-moment re-plugging reinstated the oxygen and enabled him to land safely. Engine failure caused by a faulty igniter terminated his third flight too, and an explosion in the No. 1 chamber locked the rudder and caused major internal damage. When the aircraft returned from repair in July the ignition problem recurred. Nevertheless, a dawn takeoff on August 8 was chosen for an attempt on the world altitude record, with Yeager as chase pilot.

Wearing an uncomfortable partial pressure suit which Everest described as a "portable torture chamber," a wool and nylon flying suit and thick undergarments on a hot summer morning, he climbed into the B-29A ready for the ascent to 30,000ft. White contrails were left by the lox as it boiled off during the climb, requiring a refill before launching the X-1. Everest eased into the cockpit, strapping on his parachute as he settled in. Oxygen, the bail-out oxygen bottle (never used) and the intercom were plugged in and the square door was sealed before Ridley retreated into the bomb-bay and pulled up the ladder.

Everest had 45 minutes to complete cockpit checks and ask Yeager to watch the ailerons and tailplane to check their operation. Having triggered the green "launch-ready" light in the B-29A cockpit, he

NACA's 46-063 at Muroc in 1949 with its crew chief, Dick Payne (third from left), and (left to right) Ed Edwards, Bud Rogers and Kenny Gaskins. Payne later received the NACA Exceptional Service Medal after entering the bomb-bay of the B-29A, inspecting the cockpit of the X-1A after it had been fatally damaged by an explosion and attempting to jettison its dangerous fuel load. (NASA)

felt the bomber begin a shallow dive as Cardenas built up speed to 250mph. On the count of ten the X-1 fell away like a bomb and Everest lit three rocket chambers, feeling the energy forcing him back hard into his seat. Climbing steeply to 45,000ft, he leveled out, adjusted the tailplane and let the X-1 go supersonic, climbing almost vertically on three chambers until the fuel was expended. With the fuel at a low level his thrust-to-weight ratio approached one-to-one. At the apex of the climb, which afforded Everest an unprecedented view of the earth's surface, he dived and guided the aircraft back through the Mach, with consequent buffeting as he sought the correct tailplane setting and returned to Muroc. He later recalled:

A World War II fighter ace like Chuck Yeager, Maj Frank K. "Pete" Everest checked out in the X-1 on March 21, 1949. Involved in the final stage of the X-1 program, he carried out flights that saw high-altitude performance take precedence over high speed. (USAF)

> "You accelerated so fast that it was tough to follow the flight plan to give you the proper Mach number to climb at and the proper angle to climb. This was because you couldn't see very well as the X-1 had a flat canopy. So you tried to pick the proper nose-up angle to maintain the established Mach number. When you reached a certain altitude you would try to make sure you didn't end up with the airplane vertical, otherwise it would be an out-of-control flight. Obviously, at high altitudes your elevator controls were no good so you used the movable horizontal stabilizer to try and keep the proper attitude on climb, while also trying to maintain the proper Mach number. It wasn't an easy thing to do at high altitude because the X-1 didn't respond that fast in a thin atmosphere."

Everest had reached 71,902ft – the highest for the nitrogen-system X-1. Another high-altitude attempt on August 25 showed the necessity for the partial pressure suit when it was required for the first time in an emergency. As he prepared to drop from the B-29A, Everest noticed a one-inch crack in the X-1's windshield edge, but decided to go ahead with the flight. Climbing at supersonic speed, he heard an explosion, felt his pressure suit inflate and saw that the crack had enlarged and released the cabin pressure. At 65,000ft and travelling at supersonic speed, his life depended on the pressure suit. Everest cut the engine and nosed over, but he was unable to communicate with Yeager in the chase F-80 as the suit restricted his breathing and speech to primitive grunts until he could reach denser, breathable air below 20,000ft.

This incident began the run-down of the X-1 program for the USAF as it was thought that the airplane was unlikely to reach much higher altitudes. Everest's ten flights (second only to Yeager's in number) and others by Ridley marked the end of the road for 46-062. Yeager made its final flight (launched from a Boeing B-50) on 12 May 1950 for the RKO movie *Jet Pilot* starring John Wayne and Janet Leigh. Some components were removed for use in 46-064 and the aircraft was repainted in orange for permanent display at the Smithsonian National Air Museum.

CHAPTER SIX

X-1 – THE SECOND GENERATION

The third X-1, 46-064, had the advantage in 1951 of a revised loading procedure that involved hydraulic lifts at the Bell plant and at Edwards AFB to raise the carrier B-29A or B-50, rather than the pit that was originally used. The bomber was then gently lowered for attachment of the rocket-plane. At one stage the X-1A had roller "skateboards" under its undercarriage units to assist the groundcrew in positioning it accurately beneath the B-50's bomb-bay. (NASA Dryden Archive)

Despite the success it had achieved with the X-1, Bell's finances in 1947 suffered in the post-war shrinkage in defense spending. It was a small company looking for new orders, and Larry Bell tried reviving the idea of a fighter version of the X-1 in an attempt to improve his company's fortunes. The USAF already had several other options for that role, however. Despite missing out on a lucrative fighter contract, Bell was asked to build four new X-1s following Yeager's supersonic flight. These aircraft were to resemble the first three, although there was some latitude for improvements. The most important of these was the long-delayed introduction of the turbo-pump system to replace the heavy, space-consuming nitrogen spheres in 46-062 and 46-063 and allow more fuel space to increase supersonic endurance.

The steam-driven turbo-pump for the XLR-11 engine took five years to develop satisfactorily. It was finally installed in the third X-1, 46-064, which had earned the nickname "Queenie" because of the time it had spent grounded as a "hangar queen." Identifiable by its new "strapless" windshield and white finish, it emerged three years late at Edwards in April 1951 and made its first glide flight with NACA pilot Joe Cannon at the controls on July 20. To prepare for its first powered flight, after another long delay due to a lack of funding, the airplane was loaded with propellants for a captive flight on November 9. Cannon, attempting to lock the cockpit door, hit a switch

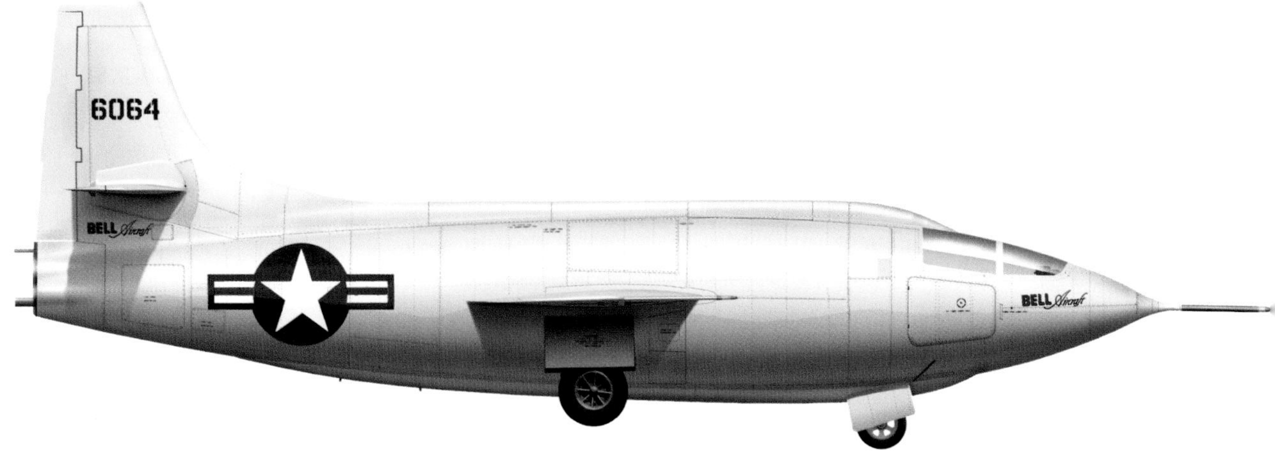

Bell X-1 46-064, Edwards AFB, California, November 1951

This aircraft was the first X-1 to have the turbo-pump fuel system, and it was destroyed at Edwards on November 9, 1951 before it could be flight-tested. After a fuel-jettisoning problem during a captive-carry flight, 46-064 was returned to base under its carrier EB-50A 46-006 and towed to the propellant loading area to be de-fuelled. As pilot Joe Cannon began the lox jettison procedure several explosions and fires occurred, destroying the X-1 and fatally damaging the EB-50A. Cannon was badly injured by escaping lox, which burned through his clothes and froze his skin. The aircraft had made only one free flight – a glide flight on July 20 – prior to its destruction. The explosion was one of several later attributed to the use of inappropriate gasket material.

and accidentally jettisoned the nitrogen (substituting for the intended hydrogen peroxide), preventing the fuel from being jettisoned before landing. A successful landing was made by the B-50 crew with the X-1 still aboard, and it was taken to the nitrogen source area to refill the tank and de-fuel the propellants.

Cannon then began the usual jettison procedure by pressurizing the lox tank. There was a small explosion, followed seconds later by a series of major detonations that destroyed the X-1 and much of the B-50 (46-006), despite immediate action by the firefighters. Cannon was severely burned by the leaking fuel as he crawled away from the disaster, blown onto his hands and knees in pools of lox by another

Nose wheel collapses became almost traditional throughout the entire X-1 program and they continued with the final example, the X-1E, which sustained damage during landing on three occasions. Fortunately, this often caused only superficial scrapes. It was necessary to pull back hard on the control column when touching down to prevent the nose dropping too fast as elevator authority ran out. Although this was a counter-intuitive action for pilots, who feared stalling if they over-controlled, it was the only way to prevent the nose-gear leg from becoming over-stressed and collapsing. (NASA Dryden Archive)

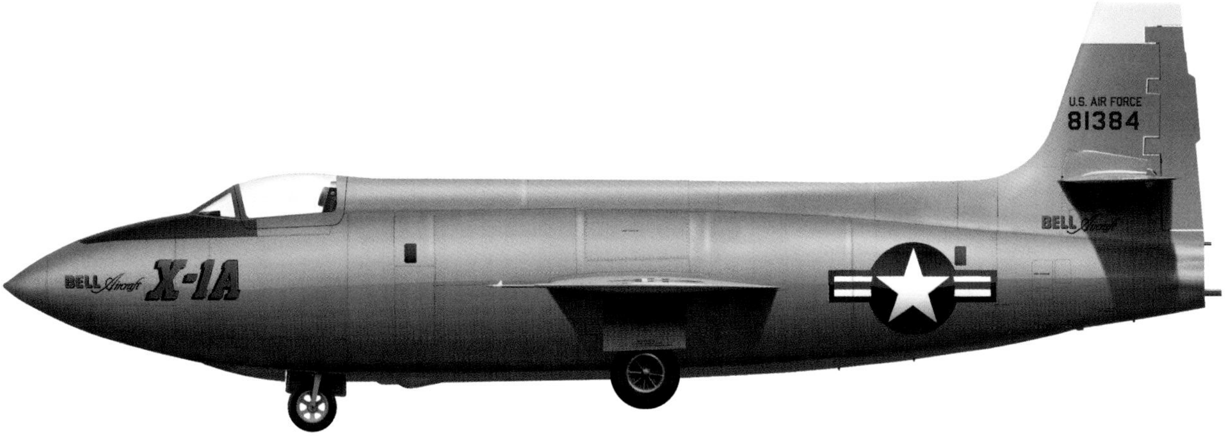

Bell X-1A 48-1384, Buffalo, New York, December 1952

X-1A 48-1384 was rolled out at Bell's Buffalo, New York, facility in December 1952 in a similar FS 12243 Gloss Orange paint scheme to that applied to the first XS-1, although this was removed before its transfer to Edwards AFB in January 1953. Modified in April 1953 by replacing its nitrogen tube bundles with spherical tanks, 48-1384 resumed tests in October. On December 12 Chuck Yeager achieved a speed record of Mach 2.44 at 75,000ft in it, but the X-1A became uncontrollable and Yeager had great difficulty in recovering it at 25,000ft. Transferred to NACA in September 1954 and equipped with an ejection seat, 48-1384 was lost on its second NACA flight on August 8, 1955 after an explosion occurred in its lox tank due to faulty gaskets just before launch from its B-29 carrier. Pilot Joe Walker was able to exit the cockpit assisted by crewman Jack Moise but the damaged X-1A, with its undercarriage extended and most of its fuel trapped in its tanks, had to be jettisoned moments later.

explosion. Two Bell personnel, William Means and Walt Myers, pulled him clear and drove him to the hospital. The cause of the explosion was unknown for four years, by which time three more aircraft had been lost for the same reason – faulty leather gaskets in the fuel system.

Ordered as MX-984 on April 2, 1948, the second-generation aircraft were designated X-1A, X-1B, X-1C and X-1D. The X-1C followed Robert Woods' original wish to develop an armed X-1. Various types of gun armament were sketched out for the nose section, and a unique set of vertical winglets above and below the wings to damp yaw was to be combined with a retractable ventral fin to aid stability. Like the other second-generation X-1s, it had a 4.5ft fuselage extension, eight percent wing (which produced 60 percent less drag than the ten percent wing at Mach 1.1), a standard control column and a conventional, jettisonable fighter-type canopy that was removable for pilot entry. There was still no ejection seat, however, and the canopy had to be locked into place once the pilot was in the cockpit. Bailing out at X-1 speeds and altitudes was still an unenviable proposition.

Entry while aboard the EB-50A was via two walkways parallel to the cockpit, which meant that the nerve-wracking ladder used with the X-1 could be abolished. The X-1C reached the mock-up stage, but jet fighter technology had advanced so fast that the well-armed F-86 Sabre and its successor, the supersonic F-100 Super Sabre (already taking shape in 1950), made it redundant. The X-1C was cancelled later in 1948.

Bell X-1D 48-1386, Edwards AFB, California, July 1951

The first and most unfortunate of the revised second-generation X-1s, 48-1386 (the sole X-1D) was taken to Edwards AFB in July 1951. It made one unpowered flight on July 24 flown by Jean "Skip" Ziegler. Its second flight on August 22 was curtailed when it proved impossible to pressurize its nitrogen system sufficiently. Pilot "Pete" Everest initiated fuel jettisoning, but an explosion occurred in the rear fuselage and he had to make a hasty exit from the cockpit. The airplane's landing gear had been forced down by the explosion, hanging 8in below the EB-50A carrier aircraft's undercarriage ground contact point, ruling out a safe landing. The X-1D therefore had to be jettisoned to its destruction over the desert.

The first of the four to be completed was X-1D 48-1386, which had a revised low-pressure fuel system and more fuel than the other three. Taken aloft in bare metal finish beneath EB-50A 47-006A on July 24, 1951, it was flown by Jean "Skip" Ziegler. He had recently joined Bell as chief test pilot after a year with North American Aviation. Initially given charge of Bell's innovative variable-geometry X-5, he made the

Jean "Skip" Ziegler climbs into the X-1A, for which he made the first six flights. The brevity of X-1 flights was reflected in Bob Champine's total flight time of 1.2 flying hours – the total outcome of no fewer than 13 flights! (Bell Aerospace)

An F-86A chase-plane accompanies the X-1A back to Edwards AFB after a 1953 flight. Jean "Skip" Ziegler and Chuck Yeager flew the 1953 tests in this X-1 variant, with Yeager taking over after Ziegler's death in the X-2. (NASA)

first and only X-1D flight – a glide that ended in a typical nose-wheel failure. After repairs it was prepared for a second flight on August 22 in the hope that it would achieve twice the speed of the X-1s and stave off competition from the US Navy's D-558-2, which had already beaten Yeager's altitude record with an unofficial figure of 79,494ft on August 15 and a speed of Mach 1.88 on August 7.

Pete Everest entered the cockpit at 7,000ft ready for a supersonic dash, with Col Boyd and Lt Col Gus Askounis flying chase. Jack Ridley co-piloted the EB-50A and Maj Wilbur Sellers (killed the following day in an F-94B Starfire accident) was the pilot. Everest immediately noticed that nitrogen pressure was down to 1,500psi and falling, and after a quick conference the crew decided to abandon the mission. This meant Everest returning to the X-1D cockpit to jettison the fuel. He stood on the seat, with Bell rocket expert Wendell Moore standing beside the cockpit, and opened the lox valve. There was a loud explosion and Everest saw fire roaring out of the X-1D's fuselage and into the bomb-bay. Its undercarriage lowered and locked, projecting 8in lower than the EB-50A's undercarriage and preventing a safe landing for them both.

In a magically co-ordinated move, Ridley reached for the emergency release handle to drop the lethal cargo before it destroyed the EB-50A too, just as Everest leaped clean out of the cockpit, over the crouching Moore and into Ridley as he reached for the handle. Ridley was knocked over, which was fortunate as the locking pins in the release shackles were still in place and the burning X-1D would have been jammed in position if he had pulled the lever. Boyd saw X-1D undercarriage parts

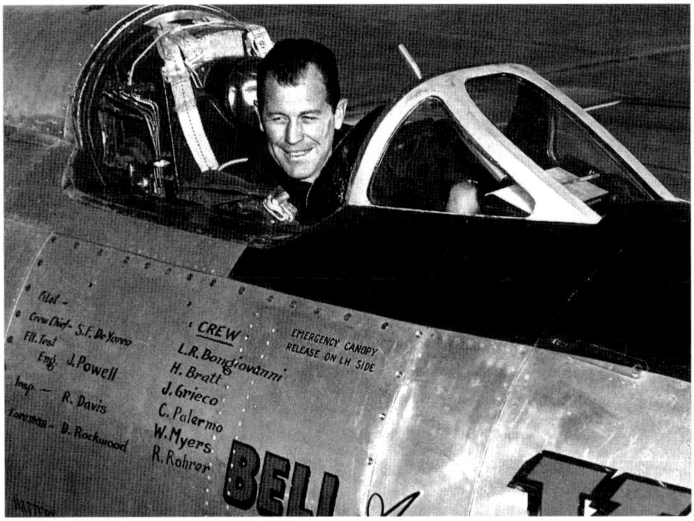

Chuck Yeager in the X-1A, which was decorated with the names of the groundcrew and a record of its flights. Yeager felt at home with the pressure dome regulators and the X-1 fuel system since they reminded him of the kind of equipment he had learned to understand as a child when he helped his father, an expert mechanic, in his work on the West Virginia gas fields. (USAF)

falling from the bomber and ordered them to drop the airplane. Ridley reached into the EB-50A cockpit and pulled hard on the normal release handle, opening the now unpinned shackles and allowing the blazing burden to fall away and smash into the desert floor a minute later. Once again, the cause of the explosion was eventually found to be leather gaskets in the fuel system. The loss of the aircraft set the X-1 program back by about two years until the X-1A was ready and considered safe to fly.

WILD RIDES

The first X-1A was delivered to Edwards on January 7, 1953, ready to continue the quest for higher altitudes and speeds to beat the US Navy and NACA's D-558-2. Everest had by then decided to focus on the Bell X-2 program, leaving the X-1A to Ziegler and Yeager. Ziegler made the

Maj Arthur "Kit" Murray in a T-1 partial pressure suit with the X-1A. He and Jack Ridley flew many of the F-86 chase missions, and Murray took over the X-1A for the three USAF high-altitude flights in 1954 when the aircraft exceeded an altitude of 90,000ft. (USAF)

first six glide and powered flights before he too was recalled to the X-2 project. The first powered flight was on February 21, 1953, and on April 25 Ziegler hit Mach 0.93 when an over-speeding propellant pump forced an early engine shutdown. On several occasions he had reached this speed and encountered the usual buffeting and aileron buzz that the X-1 series generated before slipping smoothly through the Mach. Despite reassurance from Yeager (flying on his wing in an afterburning F-86), he was reluctant to go faster and persuaded Bell to conduct static tests on it. Before he could experiment further Ziegler was killed in the explosion of X-2 46-675 while suspended in the EB-50A's bomb-bay on May 12, 1953.

Yeager then (somewhat reluctantly in view of his wife's serious illness) took over the remaining contractor flights to save training another pilot, progressively increasing the speeds from Mach 1.15 on his first flight to Mach 1.5 on the second, although he recommended an X-1 style control wheel to replace the standard "stick" as aileron forces were so heavy at that speed. The X-1A had also received nitrogen storage tanks to replace the tube bundles inherited from the X-1s. Yeager was pleased with the extra four minutes' endurance compared with the X-1 and considered the X-1A a much better aircraft, despite the discomfort of the T-1 pressure suit and the scary prospect of being locked into the cockpit pre-flight with no ejection seat. Ridley joked darkly that they would provide him with a can-opener and line his route with mattresses.

On December 8, at the start of the USAF's X-1A high-speed program, Yeager attained Mach 1.9 at 60,000ft. With Mach 2 so close, another flight was scheduled for December 12 using the established team of Ridley, Frost and Russell and flight profiles that were similar to the X-1's. Yeager and Ridley estimated that the X-1A would be stable up to Mach 2.3 at 72,000ft, at which point the tail surfaces would be inadequate. They called their plan "Operation NACA Weep" to show their determination to beat Crossfield's record, and they scheduled the attempt for December 12, several days before planned TV shows celebrating the D-558-2's achievements. Yeager got in a couple of hours of duck-hunting that morning before driving his battered, veteran pale blue Model A Ford to the high-tech X-1 facility. Lt Col Ridley and Maj Kit Murray were flying chase in F-86s and Maj Harold Russell flew the B-50.

At that point the X-1A's nose yawed to the left and the right wing rose up. Rudder and ailerons had no effect and the aircraft departed

NEXT PAGES

YEAGER'S LAST X-1 FLIGHT

The X-1A was dropped at 30,500ft and Yeager climbed to 45,000ft on three chambers, with shockwaves visible over the wings. He fired the last chamber and accelerated through the familiar turbulence at Mach 0.95, climbing a little too steeply because the blinding sun prevented him from seeing his attitude indicator. He reduced the angle, reached Mach 1.1 and pushed on with his remaining fuel, having some difficulty in holding the aircraft steady until Mach 2 appeared on the meter at around 76,000ft. Lowering the nose, he forged on through Mach 2.2 until he was travelling at Mach 2.4 – the fastest speed ever attained by the X-1 – but then lost control of the aircraft.

A coat of white paint was one of the modifications made to the X-1A when it was passed on to NACA in September 1954, but the area around the lox tank was left in natural metal. (NASA Dryden Archive)

controlled flight, entering a series of wild gyrations that slammed Yeager repeatedly against the cockpit sides and cracked the canopy with his helmet. He retained enough consciousness to shut down the motor and reflect that he had finally gone "too high, too fast, too late" as the aircraft hurtled out of control for up to 50,000ft, before finally entering an inverted flat spin. His pressure suit had inflated but his visor was fogged. Somehow he located both the rheostat to heat his helmet faceplate so that he could see and the tailplane trim switch to change the stabilator angle, although he thought it likely that his aircraft no longer had a tail. With little time left before he smashed into the Sierra Mountains, Yeager managed to control the inverted spin and the X-1A went into a "normal" spin 4,000ft later, from which he recovered at 25,000ft and pointed the tough little airplane back towards Edwards AFB.

The X-1A's record-breaking Mach 2.44 flight on December 12, 1953 was the fastest for any X-1 variant, and it was also Chuck Yeager's last X-1A flight. The aircraft went completely out of control at Mach 2.44 and 75,000ft due to inertia coupling as the flying controls ceased to have any effect in this atmosphere. The rocket-plane entered wild, spinning gyrations, during which Yeager was subjected to enormous stresses that almost rendered him unconscious. The tumbling, inverted spin continued for 36,000ft before denser air allowed the aircraft to be restored to stable flight and safely landed. The X-1A's immensely strong structure withstood forces that would have torn most aircraft apart and the only damage was a cracked canopy, struck by Yeager's flight helmet during a particularly violent contortion. His laconic comment to chase pilot Jack Ridley as he leveled out was, "Boy, I'm not gonna do that again. If I had an ejection seat you wouldn't still see me sitting in here."

ABOVE Possibly inspired by his predecessor, rodeo expert Jack Woolams, NACA pilot Joe Walker prepares to "break in" the X-1A for its first (and last) NACA flight in July 1955 – a disaster that he was lucky to survive. (NASA Dryden Archive)

He was awarded the Harmon Trophy for this wild ride, his final X-1 flight, during which he attained 1,612mph (Mach 2.44) at 74,200ft. The main outcome of this highly eventful flight was to demonstrate the need for much larger tail surfaces to avoid the phenomenon of "coupled" longitudinal and lateral instability that had so nearly cost Yeager his life.

While such redesigns were begun the USAF decided to limit the aircraft to Mach 2 and focus on reaching altitudes above 90,000ft. The X-1A made three more USAF flights, with New Yorker Maj "Kit" Murray as pilot. He beat the D-558-2's 83,235ft achieved by US Marine Corps test pilot (and ace) Maj Marion Carl with a new altitude record of 87,094ft. Murray increased this to 89,750ft on June 4, 1954, although the X-1A then tumbled out of control as it had done for Yeager, but at a much slower speed. It resumed stable flight at 65,000ft. USAF test pilots had by then developed new techniques of alternate aileron application to maintain control. Murray made a final attempt on August 26, 1954, reaching 90,440ft, thereby fulfilling the USAF's goal with statistics that would remain unchallenged for more than two years. He also remembered his wife's request to pick up a loaf of bread on the way home from work. "Kit" Murray later became X-15 project manager, worked for Bell Helicopters and lived to the age of 92.

The X-1A was subsequently transferred to NACA for further experimental work, although it only made one more successful flight following the installation of an ejection seat. On July 20, Joe Walker (a highly competent but sometimes temperamental pilot) accelerated the aircraft to Mach 1.45, at which point he encountered severe aileron buzz and had to abort the flight.

A second attempt on August 8 ended the X-1's career and almost killed Walker. Just before the drop from the B-29A, with Walker sealed into his cockpit, an explosion occurred in the X-1A's lox tank, rendering the pilot temporarily unconscious. Flying debris cracked the windshield of Murray's guardian F-86 near the B-29A's right wingtip, although the F-51 chase-plane piloted by future astronaut Neil Armstrong escaped damage. The X-1A's undercarriage extended as its doors were blown off, there was other major internal damage and it appeared to have dropped

A band of frost indicates the location of the X-1A's liquid oxygen tank as it blasts over Edwards AFB. Its XLR-11 rocket propulsion was supplied by Reaction Motors, a company that was founded in 1941 by members of the American Rocket Society. Running time between overhauls for the XLR-11 was initially just one hour, and this had been increased to 1.5 hours by September 1947. (USAF Museum)

Bell X-1B 48-1385, Edwards AFB, California, August 1955

Like the X-1A and X-1D, this variant had a 4.5ft fuselage extension (for increased fuel capacity) and a revised cockpit profile to give a "combat cockpit" in case there was any possibility of a military version being produced to perform the photo-reconnaissance mission. Maj Arthur Murray used it for a series of high-altitude flights in 1954, achieving an unofficial record of 90,440ft. In 1957 48-1385 was modified with extended wingtips to allow it to trial the hydrogen peroxide-powered reaction control system for the X-15 in its flights above the atmosphere. The system was only tested in one X-1B flight on November 27, 1957. This aircraft was one of the few X-1 survivors, making 27 flights between September 1954 and January 1, 1958, when NACA pilot Neil Armstrong took it to Mach 1.5 on the final flight for the X-1 series. 48-1385 has been permanently on display at the USAF Museum at Wright-Patterson AFB since January 1959.

TOP LEFT The sole X-1B at Edwards AFB in August 1955 after eight months of modifications at NACA Langley, where it was equipped with NACA's instrumentation in the nose bay, a conventional hinged canopy and an ejection seat. Early studies for the XS-1 included testing a side-opening canopy but it could not provide adequate strength for transonic flight. Capable, like the X-1A, of Mach 2.5 performance, the X-1B exhibited a tendency to roll and yaw above Mach 2, with the wings dipping downwards at more than 60 degrees. This deterred the USAF from exploring the X-1B's maximum speed potential and led to the installation of the hydrogen peroxide reaction control system towards the end of its flying career. (NASA)

LEFT The X-1B in July 1958 after the installation of the reaction control system, for which vents can be seen above the extended left wingtip and aft of the fuselage insignia. This X-1 variant was originally intended as an armament test-bed, using .50-cal machine guns, but that role was transferred to the X-1C, which only reached the mock-up stage. (NASA Dryden Archive)

The X-1B cockpit, which included a conventional control column, a Machmeter reading up to Mach 3 and round chamber pressure gauges, with fuel and lox dials on the center right. As X-15 pilot Robert White described it, "There was no throttle. You simply flipped a switch and held on." Controls and jettison switches for the fuel and hydrogen peroxide tanks are at the upper left. The X-1A cockpit differed considerably in detail. (Bell Aircraft Corporation)

two inches in the shackles. Walker was rapidly extricated from the cockpit and it was decided to jettison all remaining fuel and hydrogen peroxide. He courageously returned to the cockpit to do this, but it proved impossible as the nitrogen and hydrogen peroxide systems had also lost pressure, ruling out any hope of a safe landing for the B-29A while the X-1A was still hanging beneath the aircraft.

A quick conference with NACA official Joseph Vensel elicited the instruction to jettison the aircraft over the Edwards AFB bombing range. The wounded X-1A descended 6,000ft in a flat spin, exploding across the desert – another casualty of the gasket syndrome. Walker subsequently received a NACA medal for heroism.

On this occasion it was possible to reconstruct the debris and isolate the fault, with the new X-1B as a reference source. When the lox tanks and pipes were examined a greasy deposit was found and identified as tricresyl phosphate mixed with carnauba wax. Further investigation showed that this chemical was used by the Ulmer Leather Belting Company to treat the leather used to make gaskets in the lox tank. Bell investigator Wendell Moore experimented by putting tricresyl phosphate in lox, with which it united chemically, and then striking it with a hammer. He found that frozen tricresyl phosphate would explode if subjected to any sudden impact, such as the shock of sudden tank pressurization. All four X-plane explosions and losses (including the second Bell X-2) had occurred near the lox tanks during pressurization, and all used the Ulmer gaskets, with about 0.45lb of the chemical within each set of gaskets. Ulmer leather was removed from all remaining Bell X-planes, ending the problem.

It works! Technicians at the NACA High-Speed Flight Station test the X-1B's reaction control system in April 1958, using CO_2 rather than the thrusters' intended rocket fuel. (NASA Dryden Archive)

Bell X-1E

Originally built as the second XS-1 for NACA, this aircraft (46-063) was re-manufactured in 1952 as the only X-1E. It was given a new canopy, turbo-pump fuel system, an ejection seat and a four per cent thickness/chord ratio wing – the thinnest for any X-1 variant. Only the landing gear and tail surfaces remained unmodified. The airplane first flew in December 1955 and completed 26 flights before its retirement in April 1959.

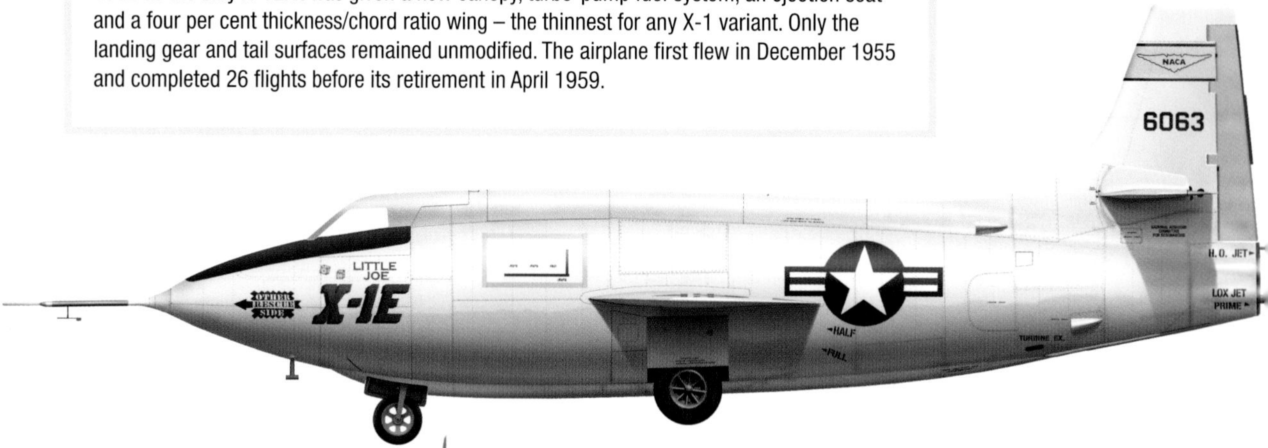

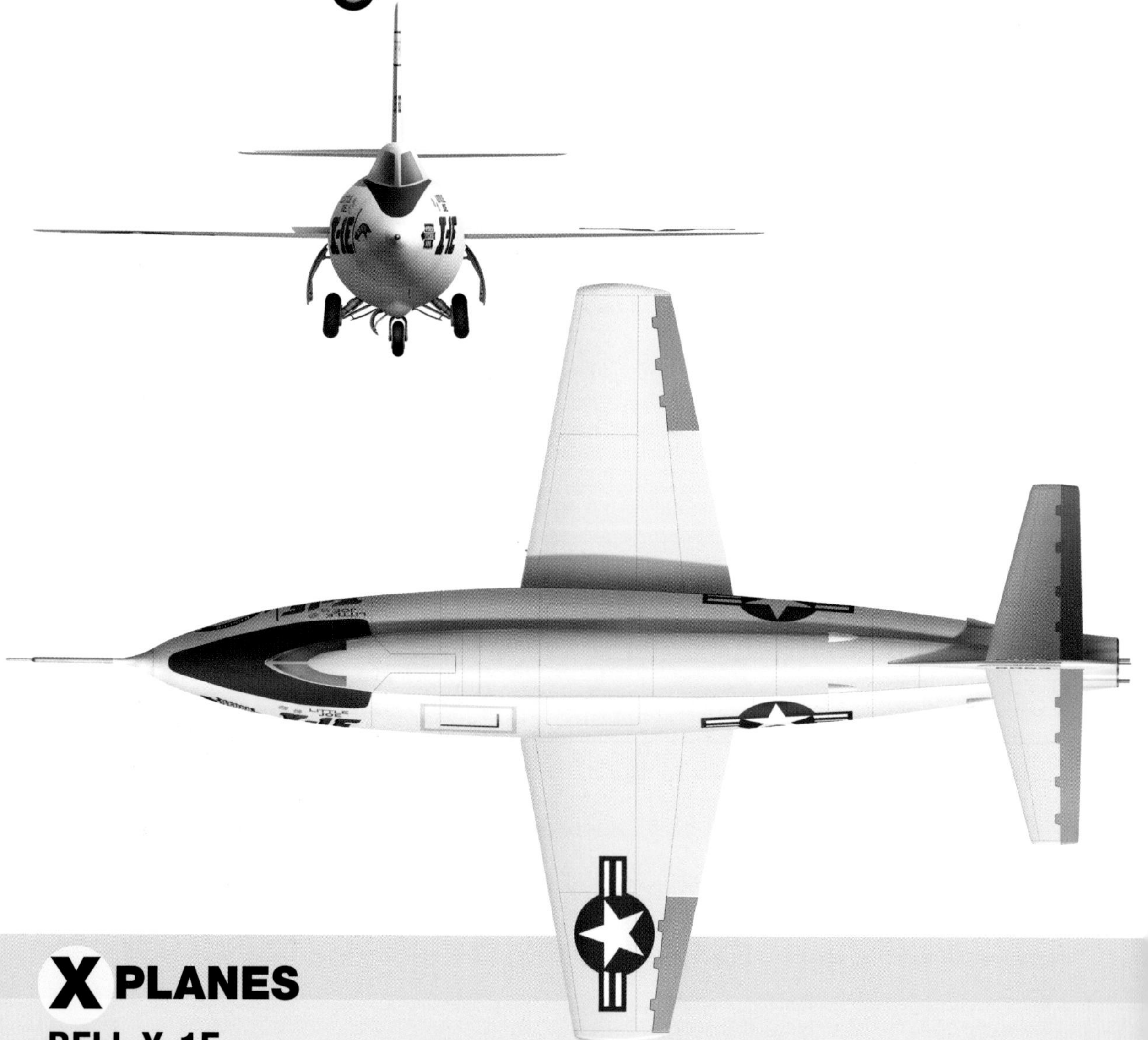

The Douglas D-558-2's more conventional one-piece, removable cockpit canopy was echoed in the design of the X-1E when it was modified from the second XS-1 by Bell and NACA at Edwards AFB. The outline of the original XS-1 transparency can also be seen. Although it was constricted, the cockpit was not as confining as that of the D-558-1, in which the tiny canopy made it almost impossible for the pilot to turn his head sideways. (Bell Aircraft Corporation)

AND THEN THERE WERE TWO

Only two X-1s remained – the X-1B, delivered to Edwards on June 20, 1954, and the X-1E, rebuilt from XS-1 46-063. The X-1B resembled the other second-generation aircraft except for a lack of NACA instrumentation. The latter would be installed when it was transferred to NACA after ten USAF familiarization flights by various pilots including Everest and Murray. Yeager had by that time left Edwards for a new assignment at Kadena AFB, Okinawa, where he was to evaluate a captured MiG-15.

On the X-1B's final USAF flight Everest drove it to Mach 2.3 at 65,000ft, coping with some serious rolling and yawing at that speed on his way to becoming the second fastest pilot at that time. The aircraft was then passed on to NACA, who used it mainly to investigate aerodynamic heating in a program that began in August 1956. By the end of July 1957 the X-1B had been given slightly extended wingtips and a basic hydrogen peroxide-fuelled reaction control system to correct un-commanded rolls, yaw and pitch-up. It used a flow-control system with small roll-rockets of 5lb to 75lb thrust in the wingtips and pitch-and-yaw rockets in the rear fuselage, operated by a small control column

NACA pilot Joseph Walker with the appropriately nicknamed X-1E. This nose-art later re-appeared on the X-15 when he joined that program. Having survived the loss of the X-1A, Walker rolled the lucky dice and piloted all but four of the X-1E's 26 flights, reaching Mach 2.24 on October 8, 1957 – the X-1E's fastest speed. The confining pressure suit and helmet are reminders of the in-cockpit constraints of those flights. (NASA Dryden Archive)

on the instrument panel. A storage vessel held 2.4 gallons of H_2O_2 fuel, sufficient for 30 seconds' thrust for each rocket axis. Although this system was only briefly demonstrated in three flights by Neil Armstrong from August 1957 through to 23 January 1958 (the final X-1B flight), it provided the basis for a fully operational reaction control system in the X-15 and in many subsequent space vehicles.

While the X-1B was being prepared for the installation of ventral fins and a new XLR-11 motor, it was found that the lox tank had serious cracks that could not be welded and its research program was terminated. The reaction controls were transferred to a Lockheed NF-104A, which Walker test-flew. In January 1959 the X-1B was preserved at the USAF Museum.

X-1E 46-063 thus became the last of the breed, having escaped retirement due to the losses of its stable mates. The airplane was fitted with an improved version of the low-pressure turbo-pump system, a US Navy LR-8 (LR-11) engine, a new cockpit canopy that resembled the

X-1B 48-1385, with its under-nose sensor probe detached and hinged canopy cracked open. The new canopy arrangement simplified cockpit entry and exit aboard the carrier aircraft. Extra fuselage length for the second-generation X-1s, suggested by Dick Frost, greatly enhanced their performance potential by increasing fuel capacity to 500 gallons of lox and 570 gallons of alcohol, increasing powered endurance beyond 4.6 minutes. (Bell Aerospace)

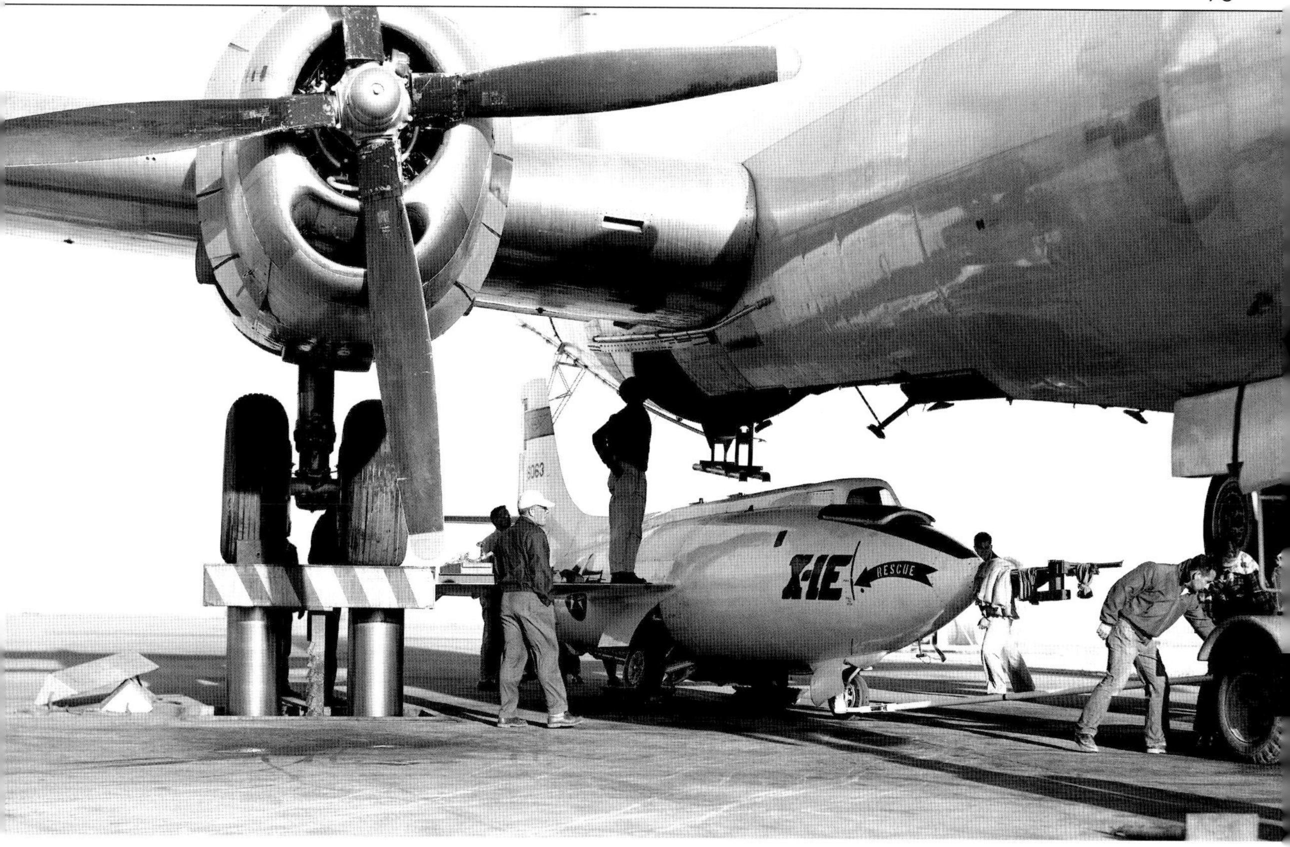

The X-1E is maneuvered into position beneath B-29A 45-21800. The "snubbers" that steadied the rocket-plane protrude from the bomb-bay above the X-1E's cockpit. (via Fred Johnsen)

OPPOSITE The X-1E is seen here strapped down for ground-running tests of its rocket motor, with numerous panels removed and groundcrew who are apparently blessed with natural noise filtering rather than modern ear protection. Even the fuelling process made a high-pitched whining noise that was audible for miles during the hours before a flight. (NASA Dryden Archive)

D-558-2's and an ejection seat borrowed from the second Northrop X-4 tailless research jet. It also received an unprecedentedly thin four percent thickness/chord ratio wing to replace the original eight percent version. The new wing, designed to enable a speed of Mach 2.5, was engineered by former Bell luminaries Robert Stanley and Dick Frost, who now ran the Stanley Aviation Corporation. It used multiple spars with tapered skins bolted on to them, while still incorporating NACA's 200 pressure orifices and 343 gauges despite a maximum thickness of 3.375 inches.

Piloted by Joe Walker, the X-1E made its first unpowered flight on December 12, 1955. Three days later the first powered flight took place. It was borne by B-29A 45-21800, just as it had been nine years before as the second XS-1. After four more aborted flights Walker took it to Mach 1.55 on June 7, and all the way to Mach 2 on August 31. Three of the next five flights were abandoned due to engine problems, and it made a hard landing on May 15, 1957 when Walker, on his last X-1 flight, was unable to see clearly through his helmet faceplate. The nose gear broke again, causing damage to the underside and main undercarriage that took until August to repair. The airplane's nitrogen cockpit pressurization was replaced by a breathable air system at this time, allowing the pilot to remove his helmet if deemed necessary.

On its next successful flight the aircraft achieved Mach 2.24 (1,480mph), and the prospect of even higher speeds due to the loss of the second X-2 persuaded NACA to install two stability-enhancing ventral fins under the rear fuselage, although they impeded maneuverability.

The highly polished X-1B cradled beneath "old faithful" B-29A 45-21800, stripped of its black undersides and Bell "stork" nose-art and decorated with a NACA tail band. With the loss of EB-50A 46-006, this B-29A reverted to its role as the sole X-1 transporter. Indeed, it was involved in all 18 NACA X-1B flights. (via Fred Johnsen)

As a stand-in for the X-2, the X-1E might have received an upgraded LR-8 working at higher chamber pressure and burning a new Hidyne/U-deta fuel that enabled it to reach Mach 3. Another hard landing on June 10, 1958 broke the nose undercarriage yet again, but the repair period required enabled the U-deta fuel supply (dimethlyhydrazine and diethylene) to be installed, together with a more powerful tailplane bell crank. While grounded in November to allow the installation of an improved ejection seat, cracks were found in the oxygen tank and it was decided to retire 46-063 – the second, but also the last, of the X-1 series.

The X-1B made 17 flights with NACA instrumentation aboard. Thirteen were piloted by Jack McKay, beginning on August 14, 1956 with the familiar nose wheel collapse on landing. The airplane was initially involved in an aerodynamic heating research program that was completed in January 1957, after which NACA initiated a series of flights to explore the use of control surfaces at high altitudes. This test program was instigated after previous X-1B pilots had reported experiencing handling difficulties due to the thin atmosphere and, consequently, low dynamic pressure on the ailerons and tail surfaces. Here, NACA technicians Lee Adelsbach and Bob Cook work on the instrument installation on June 16, 1956. (NASA Dryden archive)

CHAPTER SEVEN

X-1 LEGACY

The early X-1s had no effective means of emergency escape, but in response to reports of its difficult handling at high speeds NACA asked Bell to install an ejection seat in the X-1A in September 1954. It was tested at Edwards AFB after the aircraft's return to the base in mid-1955 – note the ejection seat rail in the open cockpit. (NASA Dryden Archive)

While Yeager's first supersonic flight was the most conspicuous achievement of the XS-1/X-1 program, the little Bell aircraft made many other contributions to the progress of aviation technology. In 12 years of systematic, practical scientific research by Bell, the USAF and NACA, they achieved a series of speed and altitude records that were far in excess of the conjectured performance of the XS-1 when it was first conceived. Their simple, incredibly strong design proved to be adaptable to several modifications, while the basic airframe and motor remained much the same at a time when jet fighter design was changing and advancing at an extraordinary rate. Bell also proved that rocket propulsion, considered too hazardous by many authorities (including NACA), could be harnessed to provide relatively safe high-speed flight when operated by experienced pilots.

Although four of the seven X-1s were lost in accidents, all were attributable to a tiny fault that defied diagnosis for years and had nothing to do with the basic soundness of the design. They proved to be incredibly resilient in other circumstances that would have destroyed most aircraft, and even their many semi-belly landings caused only slight damage. The designers of the XS-1 were, by their own admission, often relying on calculated guesswork to resolve problems for which no established knowledge of research capability could provide answers. It took years for effective computer-based design techniques to make it less necessary for pilots to risk their necks to explore the unknown.

Luck may also have played a part. The lack of an effective pilot escape system, until an ejection seat was installed in the X-1A and X-1B in 1955 for its last series of flights, was an inevitable source of anxiety for all pilots, but escape was never required. The carriage of such hazardous propellants and fuels also led to surprisingly few mishaps other than the Ulmer gasket accidents, due to the care and professionalism of all concerned in the flight programs and the thorough way in which problems were addressed, despite many consequent delays.

The hypersonic program produced the North American X-15, and for that the inter-service competition that had required both the XS-1 and D-558 to be built was replaced by cooperation on a single program managed by NACA. In the longer term came the development of NACA into today's National Aeronautics and Space Administration (NASA) and the space programs that developed from those early rocket-plane flights. Many of the early organizers of those programs, including Robert Gilruth, Hartley Soulé, Walter Williams and Neil Armstrong, all took X-1 experience with them.

The magnitude of the X-1 team's achievement was captured in the citation for the Collier Trophy, awarded by President Harry S. Truman to Lawrence Bell, John Stack and Chuck Yeager in December 1948:

> "This is an epochal achievement in the history of world aviation – the greatest since the first successful flight of the original Wright brothers' airplane, 45 years ago. It was not an achievement of any single individual or organization, but it was the result of a sound aeronautical research and development policy involving fine teamwork and cooperation between research scientists, industry and the military – a factor essential to keeping America first in the air."

INFLUENCES

Although some at Bell had retained the hope that the X-1 might have direct military applications, and the second-generation aircraft were built with fighter-type "combat cockpits" in case they might be developed into high-speed reconnaissance vehicles, the XS/X-1s were essentially pure research tools. The short endurance and fuel hazards associated with rocket power were seen as unattractive alternatives to the high-powered, long-ranging jet engines that became available by the mid-1950s. Even combined jet and rocket-powered designs like the Republic XF-91 and Saunders-Roe SR.177 were short lived as jet-powered fighters like the Lockheed F-104, MiG-21 and BAC Lightning took over the short-range point defense interception roles.

However, the XS-1's early supersonic flights cleared the way to developing a new generation of supersonic combat aircraft, and its later excursions beyond Mach 2.4 and an altitude of 90,000ft showed that airframes, pilots and control systems could survive conditions that would have been unthinkable a decade previously.

Among the X-1's structural innovations, the "all moving stabilator" (tailplane) was highly influential. Tested on a NACA Curtiss XP-42 and incorporated in the entire X-1 series, it was used in the F-86E Sabre, greatly increasing its dogfighting advantage over the MiG-15 at high subsonic speeds. It remained a secret for five years. Perhaps most importantly the X-1 program established the practice of procuring research "X-planes" that has continued to this day as the most efficient way of testing radical new designs. Defending the concept of pure research aircraft at a 1954 meeting on hypersonic flight, Walt Williams pointed out that it was six years before production combat aircraft could match the X-1's 1947 speed of Mach 1.5.

The X-1 series' thin, straight and immensely strong wing structure was very successful, and it was echoed in the design of the X-15 and combat types such as the F-104, Northrop F-5 and (to some extent) the General Dynamics F-16 and McDonnell Douglas F/A-18. It showed that swept wings were not the only way to reach Mach 2 and beyond. Thin wings were also an excellent way of avoiding transonic buffeting.

The virtual impossibility of escaping from an XS-1 in flight was a factor in the development of effective military ejection seats. Early examples were used in the second-generation X-1s at NACA's insistence, despite the weight penalty, although they did not inspire the confidence of test pilots at that stage. NACA's focus on obtaining data on supersonic control and stability was of great importance in making the early supersonic fighters safer. There were many losses early in programs such as the North American F-100 Super Sabre and McDonnell F-101 Voodoo from 1953, caused by problems with yaw and controllability at high angles of attack. Many of these were resolved through airframe redesign and piloting techniques that benefited from X-1 experience.

FURTHER READING

BOOKS

Blackburn, Al, *Aces Wild – the Race For Mach 1*, Scholarly Resources Inc. Wilmington, Delaware, 1999

Bridgeman, William, *The Lonely Sky*, Cassell and Company Ltd, London, 1956

Brown, Capt Eric, *Miles M.52, Gateway to Supersonic Flight*, The History Press, Stroud, 2012

Clarke, Jonathon, *Bell X-1. Breaking the Sound Barrier*, Cia Publishing, 2013

Cowin, Hugh W., *Research Aircraft 1891–1970, X-Planes*, Osprey Publishing, Oxford, 1999

Darling, Kev, *American X and Y Planes*, The Crowood Press, Ramsbury, 2010

Everest, Lt Col Frank Jr with Guenther, John, *The Fastest Man Alive*, Cassell and Company Ltd, London, 1958

Gorn, Michael H., *Expanding the Envelope, Flight Research at NACA and NASA*, University Press of Kentucky, 2001

Guenther, Ben and Miller, Jay, *Bell X-1 Variants*, Aerofax, Inc, Arlington, Texas, 1988

Hallion, Richard, *Supersonic Flight*, The Macmillan Company, New York, 1972

Johnston, A. M. with Barton, Charles, *Tex Johnston, Jet Age Test Pilot*, Smithsonian Institution Press, Washington D.C., 1991

Lundgren, William R., *Across the High Frontier*, William Morrow and Company, New York, 1955

Matthews, Henry, *Ziegler*, HPM Publications, Beirut, 2003

Merlin, Peter W. and Moore, Tony, *X-Plane Crashes*, Speciality Press, North Branch, Minnesota, 2008

Miller, Jay, *The X-Planes, X-1 to X-45*, Midland/Ian Allan Publishing, Hinckley, England, 2001

NASA Dryden History, *X-1 Technical Data*, NASA Armstrong Flight Research Center, 2008

Pace, Steve, *X-Planes at Edwards*, MBI Publishing, Osceola, Wisconsin, 1995

Pisano, Dominick A., van der Linden, F. Robert and Winter, Frank H., *Chuck Yeager and the Bell X-1*, Smithsonian Institution Press, Washington D.C., 2006

Rotundo, Louis, *Into the Unknown*, Smithsonian Institution Press, Washington D.C., 1994

Sands, C. D., Ed, *Pushing the Flight Envelope. The X-Vehicle Program*, Cia Publishing, 2011

Van Pelt, Michel, *Rocketing into the Future*, Springer-Praxis Books, 2012

Wolfe, Tom, *The Right Stuff*, Vintage/Random House, London, 2005

Yeager, Gen Chuck and Leo Janos, *Yeager*, Century Hutchinson, 1986

Yeager, Chuck, Cardenas, Bob, Hoover, Bob, Russell, Jack and Young, James, *The Quest for Mach One*, Penguin Studio, Harmondsworth, 1997

DOCUMENTS

Bell X-1A Pilot's Flight Operating Instructions, USAF/NACA, 1953

Champine, Bob, *Testing the First Supersonic Aircraft*, NASA Langley Research Center/Wings Magazine, 1992

Jenkins, Dennis R., Landis, Tony and Miller, Jay, *American X-Vehicles*, NASA History Office, 2003

Love, James E. and Stillwell, Wendell H., *The Hydrogen Peroxide Rocket Reaction-Control System for the X-1B Research Airplane*, NASA, Washington, D.C., 1959

Williams, Walter C., Forsyth, Charles M. and Brown, Beverly C., *General Handling Qualities – Results Obtained During Acceptance Flight Trials of the Bell XS-1 Airplane*, NACA, 1947

INDEX

References to illustrations are shown in **bold**, with the caption page in brackets if not on the same page.